ISBN 978-1-331-88564-1
PIBN 10249758

English
Français
Deutsche
Italiano
Español
Português

www.forgottenbooks.com

Mythology Photography **Fiction**
Fishing Christianity **Art** Cooking
Essays Buddhism Freemasonry
Medicine **Biology** Music **Ancient
Egypt** Evolution Carpentry Physics
Dance Geology **Mathematics** Fitness
Shakespeare **Folklore** Yoga Marketing
Confidence Immortality Biographies
Poetry **Psychology** Witchcraft
Electronics Chemistry History **Law**
Accounting **Philosophy** Anthropology
Alchemy Drama Quantum Mechanics
Atheism Sexual Health **Ancient History**
Entrepreneurship Languages Sport
Paleontology Needlework Islam
Metaphysics Investment Archaeology
Parenting Statistics Criminology
Motivational

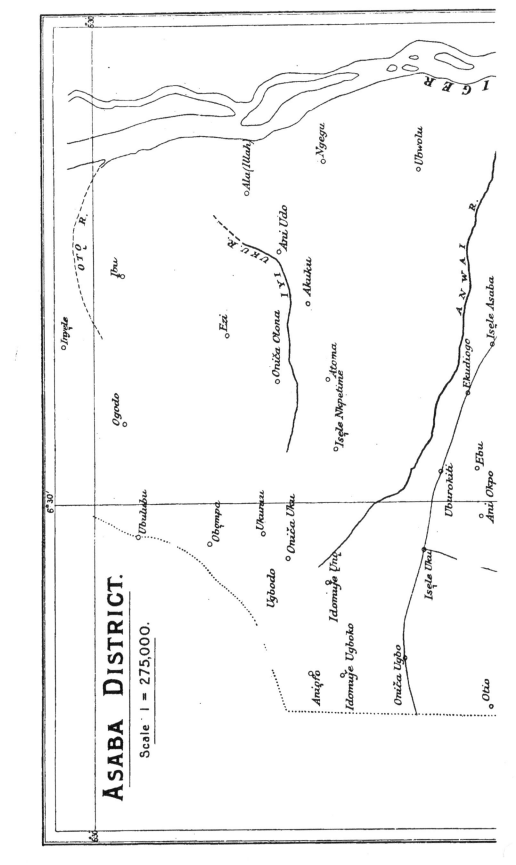

ASABA DISTRICT.

Scale 1 = 275,000.

N I G E R

A N W A I R.

OTО̥ R.

URU R.

IYI

Inyele

Ibu

Ogodo

Ezi

Onixa Olona

Ala Ulah

Ani Udo

Akuku

Ngegu

Ubwolu

Atoma

Isele Npetime

Ekudiogo

Isele Asaba

Ubulubu

Obompa

Ukunau

Onixa Ukai

Uburokiti

Ebu

Ani Okpo

Ugbodo

Idomije Unọ̥

Aniọ̥fọ̥

Idomije Ugboko

Isele Ukai

Onixa Ugbo

Otio

6°30′

5°30

6°30

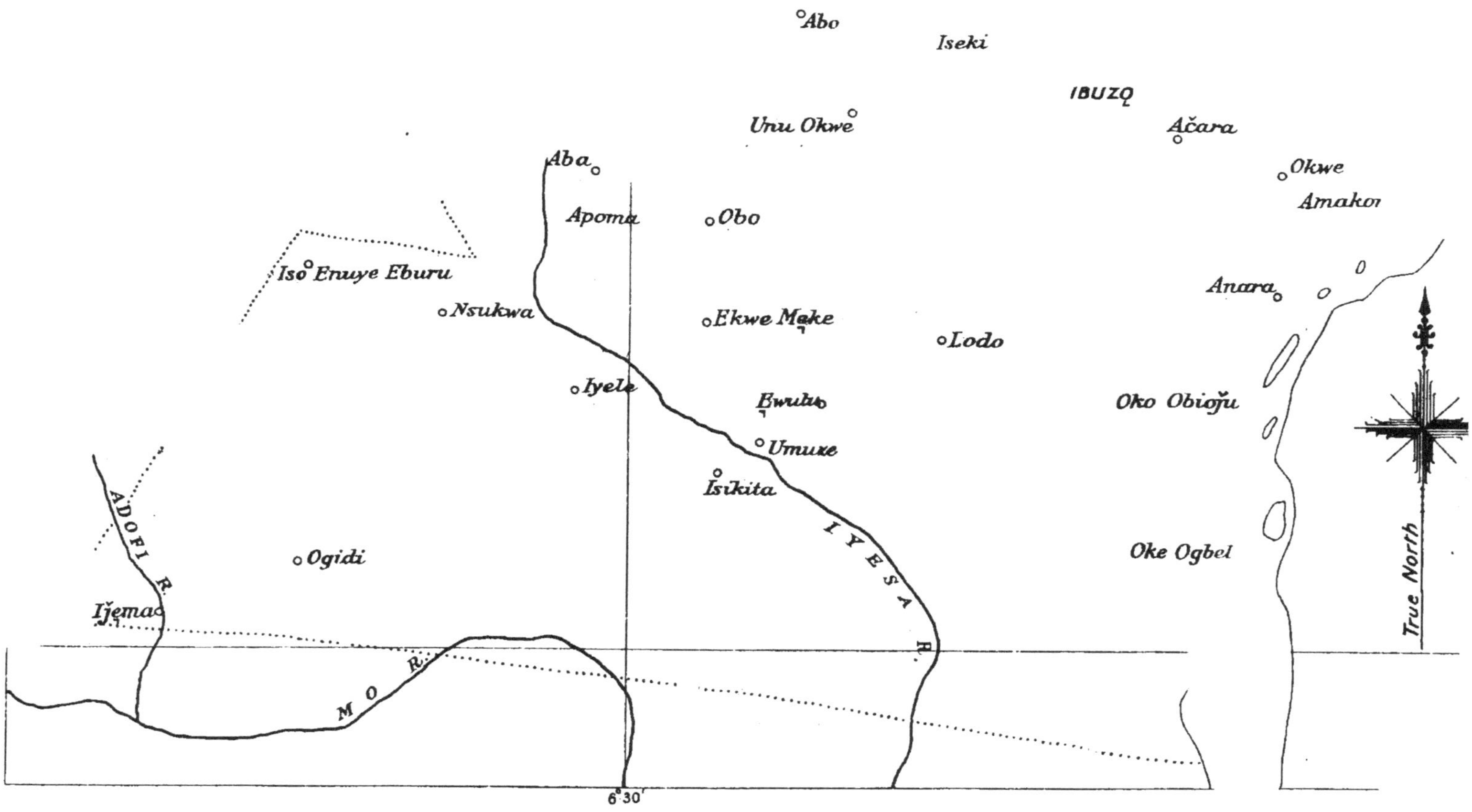
Abo
Iseki
IBUZO
Unu Okwe
Ačara
Okwe
Amakor
Aba
Apoma
Obo
Iso Enuye Eburu
Nsukwa
Ekwe Make
Lodo
Anara
Iyele
Ewulu
Oko Obioju
Umuze
Isikita
IYESA R.
ADOFI R.
Ogidi
Oke Ogbel
True North
Ijemac
MO R.
6°30′

ANTHROPOLOGICAL REPORT

ON

IBO-SPEAKING PEOPLES OF NIGERIA.

BY

NORTHCOTE W. THOMAS, M.A., F.R.A.I., ETC.,

GOVERNMENT ANTHROPOLOGIST.

PART IV.

LAW AND CUSTOM

OF THE

IBO OF THE ASABA DISTRICT, S. NIGERIA.

LONDON:

HARRISON AND SONS.

1914.

TABLE OF CONTENTS.

LIST OF PLATES.

I.—GENERAL.

THE Asaba District extends from about 6° 30′ N. to about 5° 55′ N. The western border is somewhat irregular; in the north the angle between the north and west boundary line lies about 6° 30′; from here it trends westwards nearly as far as Oweri in the Agbor district 6° 22′ west; then there is a re-entering angle some 10 miles to the south-east, and the southern boundary line is reached about 6° 23′ at Utagḅa Ụnọ. The eastern boundary line is formed by the Niger.

The southern portion of the district is in the main low, and, more especially near the Niger, swampy; in the rainy season a large area is uninhabited. A few miles behind Asaba, and from there westwards, the land rises to a height of about 400 or 500 feet, and the Hinterland of the district lies in the main upon this plateau. There are no important rivers running through the district, but the Otọ, which cuts off the Ishan town of Inyele from the rest of the district, is deep, though narrow in the dry season. Among other rivers may be mentioned the Aṅwai, entering the Niger at Asaba. It then curves northwards to Isele Asaba, and from there runs for some distance near the Asaba-Agbor road as far as Uburokiti, after which it trends northwards towards Udumuje Ụnọ.

The population of the district, according to the last census, is 200,000 in round numbers, and, although the population is fairly homogeneous, four or five distinct dialects may be dis-tinguished. Inyele, in the north, speaks Ishan, and in the south-west the people of Nsukwa, although their language does not differ markedly from their neighbours, appear, judged by the standard of customs, to belong to a different stock.

(1172)   B

In the north-west portion of the district two towns, Ukunzu and Ubodu, with an offshoot Ubulubu, are remarkable as being Yoruba islands, which appear to have settled in their present situation perhaps some 700 years ago, and yet, in spite of their isolation, preserve their Yoruba language, known as Unukumi, which resembles the Yoruba of Usehin and Akure, until the present day. In fact, the older people are even now unable to speak Ibo fluently, and it is said that until some 50 or 60 years ago the population was monoglot Yoruba. As far as the customs go, they appear to have entirely assimilated those of the surrounding Ibo, except, possibly, in burial customs. How far back this identity of custom goes, I had no means of ascertaining, as I could find no tradition relating to the change. Their own account of the manner in which they were brought from the neighbourhood of their own tribe was that they followed the first King of Benin City in his wanderings. The tradition is, in part, inaccurate, as they describe this first King as a son of the Ata of Ida. It appears, however, certain that until comparatively recent times the King of Benin City sent messengers annually to make offerings at the shrine of Ihroguda at Ukunzu. No doubt it is to this support of the powerful State of Benin that they owed their separate existence and immunity from outside influence.

A curious feature of the traditions, and, in all probability, of the actual history, of the towns of the Asaba district is that not only can they, unlike the towns on the east of the Niger, say who the founder of the town was, but very few towns are homogeneous in respect of origin. At Ala (Illah), for example, native tradition asserts that the original stock came, like the people of Asaba, from Nteje, east of the Niger; other immigrants came from Ida, whose ruler formerly claimed a considerable tract of land on that side of the Niger, and another small quarter is said to have come from Benin City. How far the latter statement is true is uncertain.

It has already been mentioned that the King of Benin sent

annual messengers to Ukunzu. His power appears to have extended at one time as far as the Niger, though Asaba threw off the yoke of Benin comparatively soon after its settlement by the Nteje stock. It has been stated that, according to native tradition, the present inhabitants of Onitsha, known to the natives as Onitsha Mili, came originally from Benin. So far as I was able to discover there is no foundation for this tradition. The original Onitsha, together with its sister towns, Onitsha Ubwo, Onitsha Uku, Onitsha Olóna, and others, seems to have been located a few miles west of Onitsha Ubwo, that is to say, some six miles from Isel'uku, until they were driven out by the forces of Benin. Some, at any rate, of these towns acknowledged the suzerainty of the King of Benin until some 70 years ago, when the annual messengers ceased to come. This was probably due to the defeat of the Bini by the Ishan, which took place about 1840, in the time of the grandfather of Overami.

In spite of the fact that the Bini influence had ceased to be active long before the fall of Benin City, the present Obi of Obol'uku at his accession, within the last few years, sent messengers to Calabar and Benin City tc obtain the sanction of the Qba according to traditional custom.

One result of this common origin has been that more or less formal treaties of alliance, as it were, exist between these sister towns. If it does not carry them so far as to bring an ally into the field in case of war, this is due less to an indisposition to help their kinsmen than to the fact that war, at any rate in this part of West Africa, was deemed impossible if the foe were more remote than one or, at most, two hours. In practice, the alliance manifested itself rather as neutrality than in any active form, and in more than one town I was assured that they never fought with certain other towns because they were kinsmen.

The district is remarkable in one way, as the towns are considerably larger than any on the east of the Niger. Ibuzọ is said to have 40,000 inhabitants, Asaba 27,000, Oboluku 20,000, and there are one or two others with more than

10,000. One-fifth of the population of the district, therefore, is gathered in about five large towns.

Towns have grown up in some cases on no definite plan. g ashi, for example, is a maze of highways and byways through which it is difficult to find one's way. Other towns, like Ala (Illah) and Onitsha Olona, are divided up by broad and comparatively straight avenues, which, if they do not form the boundary between the different quarters, are in almost every case the property of a single quarter.

In the matter of arts and crafts there is no very great diversity. There are, for example, no towns of blacksmiths, and no quarters for doctors. Pottery, however, is made only in three towns, Ewulu, Irhago, and Omodo, and the balance of the supply is imported from the Anam country, on the other side of the Niger. Fishery is, naturally, confined to the banks of the Niger. A description of the numerous methods in use will be found in Chapter VIII.

The physical type differs to a greater extent than one would expect in so homogeneous a population as seems to be found in the greater part of the district. The young man of Ibuzọ, for example, is easily recognised. Nsukwa, as might be expected, from their difference in custom and probably in origin, have a different physiognomy. There is a well-marked difference of facial expression between the men of Ezi, specially the older men, and their neighbours.

Language.—In all probability the languages of the Asaba district are becoming more homogeneous, and, at the same time, there is probably a tendency for them to become assimilated to the language of Onitsha. I was more than once informed that it would be extremely difficult to find anyone who spoke the old Asaba language. Certain points in the Asaba language, and in some of the languages of the Hinterland, such as, for example, the breathed " r," suggest contact with and influence by the language of Benin. However, on the other side of the Niger, at Nimo, precisely the same breathed " r " is found, and I also noted other tendencies, such as a change from " f " to " sh," in both places.

It has been mentioned above that Asaba traced its origin to Nteje, but no information is available as to whether the dialect of Nimo is also spoken at Nteje; as, however, they are only some eight or nine miles distant from one another, the Asaba dialect, if it has not maintained itself in its original form, has probably undergone changes at much the same rate as the language of its place of origin. It is a little singular that Asaba should now be taking over the language of its neighbour, Onitsha, on the opposite bank of the Niger, and Onitsha, as we have seen, originally came from the Asaba Hinterland, probably about 250 years ago.

As regards customs, it is clear that the Niger is a far more important boundary than the frontier between languages. The marriage customs on the Asaba side are completely different from those on the east of the Niger. (Possibly those of Onitsha may have been assimilated to those of their neighbours, otherwise we must suppose that the present form of the marriage custom is very recent.) On the other hand, the Idẹbwe custom has apparently spread down from the Ishan country, though it is only beginning to reach Asaba; this custom is, in point of fact, simply the Isomi* custom of the Kukuruku country modified by a change in the custom of residence, for the Idẹbwe remains in her father's house, whereas the Isomi wife leaves her father's family and lives with her husband, though both she and her children remain in all respects members of her father's family, except in so far as changes are introduced by purchase of the children or otherwise.

This penetration of the Ibo country by Ishan customs is the more remarkable because, in the first place, the Ibo is, on the whole, little disposed, even when he is close to a linguistic frontier, to learn the language of his neighbours. East of the Niger, for example, I found a knowledge of Ibo extending fully one day's march into the Igara country, but no corresponding knowledge of Igara on the Ibo side of the

---

* "Report on the Edo-speaking Peoples," Vol. I, p. 54.

frontier. How far the same is true of the Ishans I had but small opportunity of finding out. At Inyele, however, a number of men seemed to understand more or less Ibo, although they are cut off from the Ibo country by the river for 10 months in the year. This difference in receptivity may possibly be due to some difference in the marriage customs. It is plain that, if Ibo women do not object to go to the Ishan or Igara country, they will be likely to carry their own language with them. (I have observed that, where a father and mother are of different tribes, the children are usually bilingual.) This is a point on which I collected no data, though, from some of my genealogies, it is clear that Ibo women pass freely across the linguistic frontier, while, on the other hand, it is well known that not only women but male refugees formed a considerable part at one time of the population of Idumuje. In this connection it may be mentioned that the Igara, who have come to reside in various various parts of the Asaba district, appear to have given up their native language in most cases.

In one respect the custom of the Asaba side differs very markedly from that of their neighbours on the other side of the Niger. The titles or grades briefly mentioned in the report on the Ibo of Awka* are equally well marked, but over and above these are dignities, as they may be termed, "Onotu" or "Olinzele," ranging in number between four and sixteen (?), held, except in rare instances, only by individuals. These dignitaries act as a sort of council to the Obi, or head chief of the town, and have also large individual powers of dealing with law-breakers. From the names of these dignities it seems clear that their origin is to be sought largely, if not entirely, in Benin City. It must be remembered in this connection that the Obi of a town would himself often visit Benin City to obtain the sanction of the Qba to his succession, and that emissaries would go at more or less frequent intervals in ordinary times with

---

* "Report on the Ibo-speaking Peoples," Vol. I, p. 75.

presents for the King of Benin. This council of dignitaries seems to have acted as a check on the unrestrained power of the head chief at least in some towns. The Obi himself is, as was shown in the report on the Awka district,[*] virtually an unknown figure east of the Niger, if we except the town Onitsha Mili, which migrated from the Asaba side perhaps 250 years ago.

Side by side with Nzele there is a kind of minor chief known as Qkpala, of which there are three grades, who preside over the quarter, the Idumu (sub-quarter), and the Umunna (sept). Their functions are religious as well as civil, though we find side by side with them priests (Orhene), who correspond to the Ęze of the various Alose in the Awka district.

This superior organisation on the Asaba side is evidenced in another direction by the fact that the women, more especially with regard to the markets, are under the control of one or more dignitaries of their own sex. Nearly every-where in the Asaba district the markets are presided over by a functionary known as Qmu, who has disciplinary powers over offenders in the market, and can punish women for leaving their own markets for those of neighbouring towns, for charging more than the customary prices or for infractions of ritual prohibitions. In addition, they collect dues of various kinds, more especially for purposes connected with religion or magic, such as the making of the market medicine.

HISTORY.—In many respects the people of the Asaba side differ very considerably from the Ibo of the Awka district and apparently, so far as my observation goes, from the majority of the other Ibo also. This is true, not only with regard to custom, but more especially in respect of their traditions. East of the Niger, with the exception of the town of Aguku, it was comparatively rare to find any historical traditions, and, as was pointed out in the report,

---

* "Report on the Ibo-speaking Peoples," Vol. I, p. 8.

the town of Aguku occupies an exceptional position, and may possibly be of different origin, for they speak of the people round them as Ibo, precisely as the Asaba people refer to the people on the other side of the Niger as Ibo, and precisely as the people of Onitsha Mili, who originally came from the Asaba side, refer to the people east of them as Ibo.

Although the historical traditions on the Asaba side do not go back very far, probably not more than 400 years at most, there are few towns which cannot tell the story of their foundation. Thus Asaba asserts that it came from Nteje, in the Hinterland of Onitsha, and many, if not all, people in Asaba trace their genealogies back to Nevisi, who emigrated from Nteje. Some of the quarters of Ala claim descent from a man who left Nteje at the same time as Nevisi. Ibuzọ and g ashi claim descent from Aguku; Ọkpanam are emigrants from Uči, near Abo. All the Onitsha, Ezi, Ọbiọ, Obọmpa, and the Isele trace their descent to one town, which, according to the most reliable tradition that I could discover, was situated between Ọnitsha Ubwo and Igbodo.

Everywhere the tradition of the power of Benin City is strong; in some places objects are still preserved which are said to have been left behind by the armies of Benin. It is not only articles left behind by defeated warriors that are found in the Ibo country, but also cult objects. At Ohọmpa the obi keeps in his orhai (Pl. VIII) an object the name of which is given as ahiamọlo. This he takes to represent Osun, and it is said that the mother of the town Irere Olomo brought it from Idu. Ahiamọlo is the name by which the object is known in Benin City.

The precise limits of the suzerainty varied from time to time. Asaba appears to have shaken off the yoke of Benin; Ukunzu, on the other hand, which is a Yoruba linguistic island, maintained its identity, probably owing to the support which it received from Benin. According to the Asaba traditions, the influence of Benin was strong when Nevisi founded the

PLATE I.

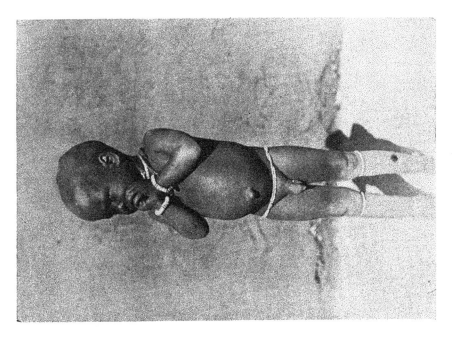

SMALL BOY (ONĬCA OLONA).

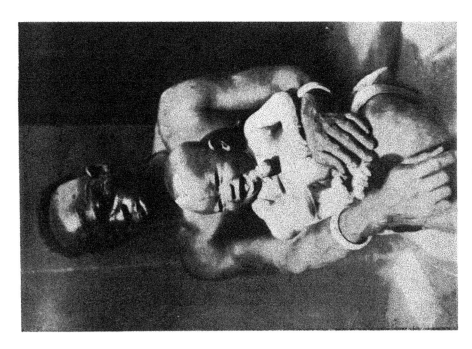

BABY (ONĬCA OLONA).

town. Onitsha appears to have crossed the Niger as a result of war with Benin City, perhaps some 150 years later.

The story told in Asaba at the present day is perhaps largely legendary, as the ground given for the emigration of Nevisi is a quarrel with his brother about the gift of a cow's tail to him by his father. According to the story, his mother had previously been sent to Ose, king of the land where Onitsha Mili now stands, and he had sent her to the Asaba side, then occupied by the town of Ačala, and the migration of Nevisi is explained by this previous visit of his mother.

After Nevisi had founded Asaba, the Ata of Ida is said to have come. His brother founded the market, and the Ata gave a wife, who was the mother of Illah, though I did not obtain any confirmation of this story at Illah. Amongst other things it is said that the Ata slept in Oye market in Asaba, and that nine palm trees grew from the nuts used to make his soup. These were cut down only about 40 years ago. It is comparatively easy to determine within limits the period at which Nevisi came to Asaba, for, according to their custom, the head of a quarter is the oldest man of the oldest generation, reckoning back to Nevisi. At the present time the oldest generation is the 8th and the youngest is the 12th, reckoning always in the male line. From this it may be inferred that the migration took place not less than 300 and not more than 400 years ago.

According to the Asaba tradition, Ado, by which name they know the mother town of the Onitshas and other places mentioned above, was driven out in the lifetime of Nevisi, that is to say, perhaps some 60 years after he left Nteje, for it is expressly stated in a tradition that Ačala called Idu (Benin City) because Nevisi and his people were getting too strong, and goes on to say that he had grand-children. Nevisi fled before the warriors of Idu, and tradition says that a civet cat and greater plantain eater walked over his tracks and concealed them. Hence these are the sacred animals of Asaba.

After the war Ačala wished to make peace with Nevisi and his family, and, if this statement is correct, it implies that his grandchildren, at least, must have been grown up. At this time the boundaries of Asaba were fixed, and, from the list of names given, it appears that neither Ibuzọ nor Ọkpanam were in existence. Another tradition says, however, that the war with Idu took place at a time when Daïke, son of the king Ezobome, great-grandson of Nevisi, was old enough to fight, and this, perhaps, is more probable. In the genealogies which I recorded, Daïke appears, and his great-great-grandson, a very old man, is alive at the present day.

Kings.—Originally Asaba had a king known as Ẹze; the first was Ezenei, grandson of Nevisi, then came Ezobome, the son of another grandson of Nevisi, then Ezago, Ago, Amarom, and Odili, but in the time of Amarom quarrels broke out owing to jealousy between different quarters who should have had the kingship in turn, and five or more men took the title of ẹze. After this the custom of taking the ẹze title spread, until now in the neighbouring town of Ibuzọ, where the movement was also taken up, 800 men have taken the title in one year. As a result of this unsatisfactory state of things the town decided to elect a head chief, and Afadie of Ajaji was selected with the title of asabwa. The present asabwa, a man of about 60, is the grandson of Afadie, who was succeeded by his second son Adanjọ, who left a son Ezogo. Ezogo did not take the title because he could not afford to make the necessary payments, and it passed to the children of a younger son. The first appointment of asabwa, therefore, dates back 100 years or more. Three kings went to Idu to have their titles confirmed, the first being Ezobome, and one king, in addition, paid dues without going. This would leave an interval of one or two generations at most before the asabwa was appointed.

The historical traditions of Asaba explain the origin of their dignitaries, such as Okute. The first is said to have been Opeči, great-grandson of Nevisi. He was sold as a slave for stealing and set free by the Ata of Ida as a reward for success in war. The Ata made him Okute, and he returned to Asaba, having in the meantime gained various magical powers. Historical tradition explains also the origin of some of the titles (see p. 54). We have already seen how the title of ẹze originated. The first title known as n̊kpese was at the outset never given to a man in the lifetime of his father. A number of men, whose names are still remembered, joined together to give the title to their sons during their lifetime, doing so in order to avoid expense. They were called dimwọ because they were expected to die as a result of their breach of tradition. When, however, they did not die, the children of other people came to them, on whose heads they put eagles' feathers to show that they were free born. The descendants of those dimwọ still have certain rights; their children pay nothing but yams for their title while other people have to pay £5. It is said that a man can become dimwọ by payment of £50 to £70, and he can then give the title of n̊kpese to his umunna.

ALOSE.—As regards the position of the alose there is comparatively little to add to what has been said in the previous report. On the whole, perhaps, there appears to be a somewhat more personal element in the alose of the Asaba district, for, with the exception of the ani, the names are usually personal. On the other hand the natives appear to be much vaguer in their ideas on the subject of the alose, for I was told more than once that all mwọ were alose. Perhaps the most interesting point was one which came out spontaneously. A man was talking to me on the subject of medicine (Pl. IV), by which is meant the magical objects which are employed to keep people alive, to protect crops, and so on, and went on to say that when they had had medicine for a long time it became alose. How far this implies a corresponding personalisation of what may at one time have been regarded as impersonal, it is difficult to say. The case is interesting inasmuch as it almost exactly bears out the view which I expressed in the " Report on the Edo-speaking Peoples," vol. I, p. 26.

It is of interest to note that in the Asaba district certain alose are attached to certain quarters, so much so, in fact, that a man cannot become orbene unless some relationship of this sort exists between him and the alose. This may be either through his father or through his mother, for when a woman comes to her husband she brings her own alose, at any rate after her mother's death; even before the death of her mother the child takes a portion of the earth from the pot representing the mother's alose and transfers it to her own house, and this is considered to be sufficient to enable her to offer sacrifice. The alose, however, is not regarded as transferred.

Many of the forbidden animals of the Asaba district are,

PLATE II.

ORHẸNE (PRIEST) OF ONIRHE AT ASABA. See page 13.

at the present day, associated with the alose, and it is an interesting question how far this association may be regarded as primary. If these animals have not come to be connected with alose through a natural tendency to bring all sacred objects into relationship, it seems probable that true totemism does not exist, if we define totemism as a primary and not a secondary relationship. In this connection it is important to notice that where a stranger has resided in a town and subsequently removes again, although he may not take the alose with him, he so far remains in relationship to the alose that he practises the prohibitions observed by the people of the town which he temporarily inhabited.

Orhene (Priest).—As in the Awka district, there are priests to whom are entrusted the cult of the various alose, but the fact that there is an alose in a town does not necessarily imply that there is an orhene there, for the orhene is not selected, but inspired to become a priest. Only in certain cases, such as the cult of the ani or earth, is there a regular functionary, and in this case the ọkpala of the ẹbo, or some similar person, takes the place of the priest on the Awka side.

The orhene (Pl. II) of Onirhe at Asaba described to me how he came to take the position. Before he began." prophesying," Onirhe used to come to speak to him and told him of things which were going to happen, such as cases of drowning, but when he turned to look the voice came from another side. One day, however, when he was sleeping, Onirhe came upon him suddenly : he saw nothing, but heard a voice. It "took" him, and he followed it as far as a point above the Niger associated with the cult of Onirhe ; there he fell into the water, picked up a stone, and came home again ; this happened some eight years ago. He went on to say that the stone which he picked up he put on his head, and where it fell off his umunna built a house for him. He went four times to collect stones, and after this experience he was forbidden to wash for three months or more, until he had regularly associated himself with the company of the orhene by the ordinary method of gifts of food.

The orhene of Ogugu at Asaba is known as Onyǫbo, and his position is hereditary. The present one is in the eighth generation from Nevisi, and is great-great-grandson of Opeči, the first Onyǫbo who, it will be remembered, is said to have acquired magical powers at Ida. These are still associated - with his descendants, and when rain does not fall, a doctor divines in order to decide, and the Onyǫbo has to offer to Ogugu. He receives one yam from every inhabitant in Asaba, which is brought and offered to arǫ, the year.

At Onitsha Olona I received an account from Mokweni, the orhene of Nkpetime, of how he came to take the office. His father and grandfather had been orhene before him and after his father, his father's ṅwago. It is a rule that if the own son does not succeed, the ago (see p. 20) does so, but this apparently does not exclude the necessity for some sort of religious experience as a preliminary. Mokweni said he went to farm when something pressed him down to the ground and he answered " oh." Nkpetime then said he must become orhene and offer her sacrifices. He did no more work in the farm that day for his eyes " turned " and he began to answer (ǫzamwǫ). He saw Nkpetime, who wore no clothes and was like a white man.

Nkpetime is commonly regarded as a woman; she is said to live in a shallow pool, largely overgrown, known as Nkpetime, not far from Onitsha Olona. I have been assured by educated natives that they have seen some object, which was not a manatee, in this pool, and that it resembled a woman : it answers to the ordinary description of a mermaid and appears to be known in Lagos as "mammy water." Custom requires that the orhene shall go to this pond annually three days after he has gone into "nzu" and swim in it after making certain offerings. I was in Onitsha Olona at the time when he should have done this but did not accompany him, and he told me on his return that he has now got an old man and if he tried to swim, Nkpetime might have taken him, so out of consideration for his family he refrained from his annual plunge. He appeared to have been in a trance-like

PLATE III.

Leopard.

Cross roads.

Mirror.

3. Ubido (tiger cat).
2. Moon.

1. Seat.

5. Nkpetime.
4. Sun.

QBWQ OBODO, FIGURES DRAWN ON THE GROUND FOR THE CULT OF NKPETIME. See page 15.

condition during a portion, at any rate, of his time at the pond, for I could not get any connected account of what he had done.

At Iwaji, the festival of New Yams, the orhene "goes into nzu (chalk)." The women of two of the quarters rub his house, the roof is repaired, and his compound swept; in the night young men dance. After four days the orhene comes out and they beat a drum and dance before the mwọ in the evening. A woman makes figures on the ground (Pl. III), called ọbwọ obodo, with charcoal, chalk, red mud, and ashes. These figures represent amongst others the following: a leopard, tiger cat, duiker, spitting cobra, fowl, squirrel, pangolin, monkey, viper, the sun, the moon, Nkpetime. At some time during the ceremonies the orhene throws the horn of an animal, called obolo mili, which seems to be a situtunga, into his yard with two hands. If it falls crossways the ground is good, if not, there is evil in the town. When the orhene is "in nzu" no one is allowed to make a noise; quarrelling is forbidden and firing of guns.

An orbene forbids (see Glossary) what Nkpetime forbids, and says that Nkpetime is his či (p. 19). He cannot kill a spitting cobra, but must grind chalk and salt and throw on it. The leopard, monkey, squirrel, and bush-buck are also forbidden. Neither ducks, goats, or fowls may step upon the figures drawn upon the ground. He may not drink palm wine for it would kill him.

All the ọkpala are cleansed before Ibanzu, and none of them may see another during the whole of the three days, nor wash for sixteen days. After washing they come before nzu and offer kola.

At Obuluku I was told that the orhene always gets his alose from his mother, grandfather, or grandmother. If a son is born of a mother from an ẹbo that owns the alose, but married into one that does not own it, he must return to his mother's ẹbo to become orhene.

At Nsukwa I got another account from an orhene. Nine years ago a water alose chose him; he shouted in his sleep and walked into the water. The alose brought out a flat dish, such as is used for kola, and gave it to him; he saw the alose, who was like a man. Now when the alose speaks to him he cannot see him, because he comes to him in his sleep.

Nsọ.—As was the case in the Awka district there are a large number of ritual prohibitions. The essential feature of a ritual prohibition is that it is not only forbidden, for this is also true of theft or assault or other acts forbidden by what may be called the ordinary law, but also entails ceremonies of expiation or purification before a normal state of things is restored. It must not, of course, be forgotten that the religious life is very closely bound up with the ordinary life of the people, and that even where ritual prohibitions are not in question, considerations of religion may play an important part, but from a certain point of view ritual prohibitions stand apart, and it often happens that the method of removing or varying already existing prohibitions is entirely different from the procedure adopted in the case of changes in the ordinary law.

Some of the prohibitions are of the utmost importance in the social life of the people, such as, for example, those which deal with the regulation of marriage; others are, from our point of view, trivial in the extreme. But from the native point of view, as far as one can judge, there is little or no difference of grade, though doubtless if it were proposed to make any changes in the nsọ, it would be far easier to change those prohibitions which appear to us to be minor ones.

As in the Awka district these prohibitions may be classified into prohibitions which concern husband and wife, prohibitions which deal with the relation of the sexes, prohibitions such as those which relate to certain animals and other general prohibitions incumbent upon the whole of the ẹbo, and, though they are not so important here as on the other side of the Niger, prohibitions which refer to the acts of certain animals. It is impossible to deal with these prohibitions in detail, but one or two examples of each kind may be mentioned here. ' When a woman goes to her husband's house she puts her či (p. 18 *sq.*) in a dish known as ǫkwači. If a husband gives this back to his wife, it is equivalent to a divorce, even if the act is done in haste. If the husband wishes to take his wife back, it may involve a separation of three years and various sacrifices, before atonement is made. In Asaba a runaway wife is forbidden to return if, after her husband's death, she does not succeed in coming back to shave his head.

The prohibitions regulating intercourse between the sexes depends upon the degree of kinship between the parties concerned. At Asaba, for example, if the mothers of two men belong to one idumu, the male children of the latter are forbidden to commit adultery with each other's wives ; but other acts which would be forbidden to those less nearly related, are permitted. They may, for example, take a knife (nkoti) or any other object from the woman's head. They may sit upon one mat, and so on. In some cases they are permitted to salute women in certain degrees of kinship to them, or married to certain kin of their own, by the title of " my wife." This may be done at Isele Asaba if they belong to the same ǫbo, or if they are not more than four generations removed from a common ancestor ; the use of this term of address does not imply any further rights over the woman in question.

If there are two exogamous units in a community, it is forbidden to say to a woman married into one of them that the speaker thought she was married into the other, and it is equally forbidden to call her the wife of a husband from whom she has run away.

As examples of prohibitions incumbent upon the whole community the most conspicuous case is the animal or animals forbidden by the whole town or to certain quarters. Asaba, for example, forbids civet cat and greater plantain eater, and a story is told to account for this prohibition which closely resembles the ordinary etiological totemic myth (see p. 9). At Obǫmpa, if a man and his wife go to the house of the head chief, it is forbidden to both of them to suggest that it is time to go, they have simply to get up and leave.

Some of these prohibitions refer particularly to women. In Asaba a woman is not allowed to abuse people while she is cooking, nor may she mention a vulture. Others are imposed only on the wives of certain men; at Isele Asaba a woman married to a man who has taken a title may not tie a cloth with a fringe to it.

Other prohibitions refer especially to the men who have taken a title. An ẹze may not, for example, see a corpse, nor have his cap knocked off. Some classes of doctors may not see their blood spilled on the ground.

As regards prohibitions relating to animals, these relate more especially to the market. A cock may not crow nor a dog bark, on the penalty of instant death. In the same way a cock is forbidden to fly up to the roof of a small hut which a blacksmith uses as his forge, whether the blacksmith is there or not. If it does, it pays the penalty of its rashness provided it can be caught.

From a practical point of view the most important prohibition is that which forbids the keeping of twins. Although the native will usually state that twins are not killed at the present day, I have rarely, if ever, noted a case of twins in my genealogies, except with the addition that they are dead. In one case at Ala a woman was stated to have borne twins four times, and all had been exposed in the ordinary way. Here, as in the Awka district, the recognised method of changing these customs would be to sacrifice to the ani and the mwọ, and to declare that henceforth the custom was abolished. The ọkpalẹbo would probably be the person to perform the sacrifice.

REINCARNATION.—In the account of the peoples of the Awka district it was explained that a dead man is believed to be reincarnated in one or more of his descendants or relatives. On the Asaba side the belief exists in more than one form; but in some places instead of having a dead man as či* they

---

* " Report on the Ibo-speaking Peoples," Vol. I, p. 31.

take a living man, and consequently there can be no question of reincarnation. In addition to či a man has also ẹrhi and two forms are distinguished, ẹrbi ụnọ and ẹrhi oifia. Both the name and the belief are curiously reminiscent of the Edo belief in e hi o w a and e hi o h a.*

It is said that a man before coming into the world again decides what he is going to do in his new life. At Ọkpanam they say that a person can fix before his or her death where they will return in the next life, and a woman who has married into an ẹ bo may decide to be reincarnated in a child born in that ẹbo. (It must be remembered that women are usually buried in their own country and that reincarnation depends to some extent upon the locality of the burying place.) If a man has seven wives, he may decide that he will have only one in the next life as they are too much trouble.

At Obuluku the belief is somewhat different. Here it is said that not the man himself but his či decides what his life shall be, and this is held to explain why some men are lucky and others unlucky. A man without wife or children has obviously had a bad či.

The ordinary way of deciding who is the či of a new born child is for the doctors to divine. At Onitsha Olona when the doctor comes to b w a a g o, i.e., discover the identity of the child, the father takes pieces of ẹbwo which are known as u t e. As he hands each to the doctor he names an individual, and the doctor divines for each separately.

At Ibuzọ a doctor is called upon to divine before a child is born. The husband gets o g u (u t e) from a plant called u l u o i b o for the purpose of divination and before the doctor proceeds to enquire, the father asks whether he will live till the child is born. If the diviner says he will not do so, the first duty of a doctor is to find an a l o s e or m w ọ which will hinder the catastrophe.

At Obọmpa a či is assigned to a child when it is two or

---

* "Report on the Edo-speaking Peoples," Vol. I, pp. 39 and 40.
c 2

three years old, but here the conditions are complicated by the fact that one of the quarters took living men as či and other quarters have begun to follow their example. Here it is held that the či must be someone of the same ẹbo, though a woman who marries into it reckons as one of the ẹbo.

At Ubulubu, under ordinary circumstances a či is not divined till the child has two upper and lower teeth. If the či troubles the child and makes it sick, the teeth may be marked with chalk on the lips and then the doctor is called to divine. Here a living man is či and the dead man is called on y e bi o w e, the one who comes to the world. A doctor says before the child is born who will be the o n y e bi o w e. There are no restrictions as to locality from which the o n y e bi o w e can come. In one case that came under my notice a man told me that his o n y e bi o w e came from the Ishan country, of which his father's mother was a native.

At Ezi the či of all the children born during the year are discovered before the annual worship of či. Here the či and the o n y e bi o w e seem to be the same person, for they say that a child that comes back is the či of the new child.

At Asaba the či is a dead man and the child is called his a g o ; the person reincarnated is usually of the same i d u m u or ẹbo, but may also be a friend; in one case a white man is said to be the či of the child of one of the chiefs. That the Asaba belief is actually one in reincarnation seems clear from the fact that if several children die at an early age one after the other, the husband cuts up the body of the one that dies last and buries it. When another child is born it has marks of a cutlass upon it and fears to die again. In the same way the reincarnation of a hanged man always turns his eyes up.

The reincarnation may be male or female, and there can be more than one reincarnation of the same person of either sex. The belief is, however, not quite consistent, for the same informant said that a man's či is in o w a m w ọ, the world of spirits, and receives sacrifices in order that he may protect his ago ; but he went on to say that where a man who was bad in the former life opens his eyes for the first time in a new life, as soon as he sees the world into which he has been born, he says to himself: " It is the same world I did so badly in before," and promptly dies.

An alose as well as a dead man may be či, but unlike the Awka belief the Asaba people do not hold that a tree can be reincarnated. If an ǫji seed falls into a pot used to represent či, and grows, people may say that ǫji is his či, but the man himself knows that an alose (or human being) is really his či. The či is usually represented by a pot ; some people take a pot and call the či to come inside, others use a stone. Another informant told me that a man's či follows him, and when a man entitled to carry an ivory horn meets him and holds out his horn in salutation, it is really his či whom he is saluting.

At Ǫkpanam a man can return as male or female as he chooses. He can be či to only one person though an alose may be či to several. Among the alose mentioned were Atekbe, Ogugu and Obǫsi. Those who break a ritual prohibition cannot become či, they die at once and become ajǫmwǫ (p. 28). Here, as at Asaba, the ordinary representative of či is four pieces of ębwo put in an ǫkwa (wooden dish). When a man dies his či is thrown away.

At Onitsha Olona the či must be a living person. When the či is selected by a doctor the child's mother goes with chalk and kola to the person selected ; a woman may be the či to a boy or a girl. When the ago grows the či gives it a goat ; when the či dies the ago has to bring dues and take part in the burial ceremonies ; even a small child can become či. Four pieces of stick are cut in the lifetime of the či and are kept in an ǫkwa, but this only when the ago builds his own house. A girl gets it as soon as she goes to her husband ; an idębwe (p. 78) gets it as soon as she has borne a child. At the death of the ago the four pieces are cut from end to end and thrown away. They say that ęrhi is the same as či and " follows a man from ǫkwa."

All the dead are in ǫkwa and all the people that are coming into the world. Dead people come back just as seed comes back.

The other ẹrbi they try to send back, so that a man may be prosperous a good ẹrhi is brought to a man's house. In order to effect this two baskets of yams, containing five and seven respectively, a tortoise, and other articles are provided; and an ants' nest is put in an odala tree which is bearing fruit, or an ụgili tree. They strike the tortoise with wood and tell the ẹrhi that they cannot strike him in the same way. Then its head is cut off under the tree and put in the basket with chalk, etc., and left where the doctor says it is to be put. A certain seed is chewed and spit over the right shoulder, then the ants' nest is brought to him and put down by the doctor. The ants' nest is ẹrhi.

At Ala the či is always a dead person and it is possible for one to have a multiple ago; some či come from the world of alose, Onoku, Ǫbǫnku, and others. When a woman is married she gives her okwa či to the conductors; on arriving at her husband's house she puts it in his orhai, or big medicine, till she gets her own house; then she takes it before ẹrhi (an image of mud near the wall). Before making it she calls či to come and puts chalk beside it; a doctor tells her what to sacrifice.

At Ibuzǫ an alose, such as Obǫsi, Onirhe and Ogugu, may be či of a child. If Obǫsi is či it comes to the mother in the form of a snake; when people come the snake disappears. A doctor will say which alose is či of the child and the mother must forbid (see Glossary) the same things as the alose as long as she is pregnant or suckling the child; if the mother dreams of swimming, that is a sign that the child comes from a river alose.

When a child begins to walk they make an image of či and kill a fowl to it. When a child grows up they offer whatever či demands. A woman takes či with her to her husband's house, but if her husband dies she breaks her old či and usually does not get another until she gets

PLATE IV.

CHILD ONE DAY OLD (ONIČA OLONA).

MEDICINE (CI UMWAKA) AT ASABA.

another husband. The či of a runaway wife is thrown away. When a man dies his či is thrown away and they say that the či has taken the person away whom he brought.

When a man is grown up and has a large family he may get erhi. He makes a mud image and sacrifices a goat, saying: " I put this image because you helped me." When the man dies a goat is sacrificed and the image thrown into the bush. The head wife may get erhi and puts it near či. They say that there are two či, one of which comes to hinder the other, but no clear distinction is drawn between erhi and či. They may even go so far as to say that erhi is ago (p. 20). The good erhi is erhi uno, and erbi oifia misleads him.

· If erhi oifia is not driven out when a man dies he goes to the ebe dinjọ (place of the bad), which was interpreted to mean bush. As, however, I detected traces of Christian influence in the information supplied to me by pagan natives, I am disposed to think that the ebe dinjọ is a European importation. To drive out erhi oifia an ants' nest is covered with a pot near the house, and the man makes at the same time the promise to perform the proper ceremony if he gets rich. If his life is a hard one he leaves the nest in the bush, if he is successful he brings to his house and makes erhi uno.

When a man's wife is pregnant a white ants' nest, which is to be found as soon as pregnancy is discovered, ripe and unripe nuts, a tortoise, chalk, and other objects, are put in the bush in the evening and left there till the seventh month. The tortoise is killed and put in the basket and the nuts and ants' nest with it. A small stage is made in the street, in the case of a woman living with her husband, in the direction of her own quarter. At dawn the woman washes, dresses, and chalks her eyes. A doctor brings cowries to wash her hands and puts some in the basket. An ọmu aja is plaited, i.c., a basket of palm leaf for offerings, and put on the top of the basket, and then mashed yams. If a vulture eats the yams the omen is a good one. While this is being done they sing, "Ẹrbi kwe kwe kwe, ẹrhi kwẹl'ṅkwe, ẹrhi ẹrhi bia gẹlie, ẹrhi lia, kena na ololowe," and so on, "ẹrhi agree, ẹrhi agree, come and eat, eat and go, go to ololowe (the place of the mwọ)."

At g ashi či may be a living or dead man or woman. If it is a living person the child gives a fowl to him, or her, which is offered to the či of the či. When the či dies the ṅwago sends cloth and makes an image of či in his house. One person can be či to any number of children; an alose may be či. They do not know where dead people go to, but they say a či must come to the world again; but či "means" that the child is coming to the world through him, or her, because they loved each other. There must have been some previous arrangement between them before the child came to the world and got a či.

Ẹrhi is said to be just like či and they distinguish ẹrhi ụnọ and ẹrhi oifia, which they send to join the uke that lives in the bush. For ẹrbi oifia a small house is built in the bush and a mud image made. After the sacrifice the image is thrown away and the house broken down. They think that ẹrhi is mwọ, otherwise they could not sacrifice to it.

At Obuluku a či is said to be the one who created a man. One of my informants told me that his grandfather is his či, but that he is not the same as his grandfather; či must be one related to the umunna and must be a dead person. A woman's či is represented by a mud image, a man's či by ọfọ. Či and erhi are said to live with Čuku before they come to this world; if a child tells what it saw among the mwọ they expose it in the ajoifia ("bad bush"); if it speaks before it opens its eyes its fate is sealed.

A man may be či to four or five at the same time; when the last of them dies the či is said to stop; it sits in the other world and is a mwọ. Some people have alose as či, Obira, Amaei, or Osebluwe, in any case all have an

OSEBLUWE ; ONOKU (OKPANAM).   See page 25.

image of Osebluwe (Pl. V), because Osebluwe, ẹrhi and či are said to have created the man. An alose itself, however, does not become the či, properly speaking; the real či is the orhene (priest) of the alose.

Či is put before ẹrhi ụnọ which they obtain after driving away erhi oifia. It has been mentioned above that the coming of a vulture to eat is a good omen. I found the same belief at Idumuje Uboko, where the appearance of a vulture during the worship of či is regarded as satisfactory. The ẹrhi or či is said to have come in order to eat.

At Ukunzu the či, known as ọlọ in Unukumi, is a living person, and the image is made only when they die. Či in this town appears to be rather one of the titles and the cost of making či is considerable. Here, too, fufu and oil are put out for the vulture to eat, and this is given as a reason why they never eat vultures. An image of the či is made inside the house, a stone in the river being put inside, with one snail in front and one behind. The candidate goes outside and others come and cover the snail and stone with mud and pour water from the Niger over it, saying that good things must fill his hands as the Niger cannot run dry. Then the candidate breaks a kokonut, pours some of the milk on the či, and drinks the rest. Near the image he grows an ọbọ tree, so that, just as the ọbọ grows and bears seed which different birds come and eat, his či may get many children for him. There may have been some vague idea that the ọbọ brought children for the man, but I did not satisfy myself on this point.

At Obọmpa the doctor names a dead man, who is variously said to have entered the new-born child or sent it to the world. The Uboba quarter had to take a living man as their či, and now the other ẹbo have offered kola to their mwọ and said that they, too, would have living men as their či, for the či is a source of benefit to the child, as he can give him a goat or make title for him; when a girl marries she can beg her či or ṅwago for anything that she likes.

A child's či may be another wife of his father and a father or mother may even become či to their own child. People will then say : " You do not allow anyone to help you get this child." A brother may become či to a brother. Some light is thrown upon native beliefs with regard to či by the saying that the child which one should have borne is one's ṅwago.

At Ubulubu, where a living man is či, a child is carried by its mother to the annual sacrifice to the mwọ with kola and other offerings which are put upon the či of the či. Seven ọko are given to the child's mother and chalk from the či is rubbed on the child's head. If the či is a doctor and the child is to become a doctor, the či marks one eye with chalk and then the child pays no money when he takes the title. The ṅwago can bury a či who has no children and take his property. A či must be of the same ebo. If a man's či has done ill in this life his ṅwago may suffer from the ill will of those who have been injured by his či. The ṅwago must offer a sacrifice between two cross roads so that all who wish may come and eat. If a man has been cursed before Ogugu, which is done by putting down chalk on either side of the path and striking the matchet on the ground, his ṅwago must offer to Ogugu as the killer of his či.

Two points remain to be noticed with regard to the position of the ṅwago. At O ọ pa it is forbidden to marry into the umunna of a woman who is a man's či, though he may marry into her ẹbo. If two people have the same či they cannot marry, but a brother or sister may marry the ṅwago of their sister or brother. The children of umuago are forbidden to marry.

Under ordinary circumstances children follow the prohibitions of their father and mother; it often happens that they have to take over the prohibitions of their či; this is the case at Asaba and Ala; those who have an alose as či forbid what the alose forbids. Curiously enough the rule is not the same with regard to onye bi owe (p. 20), whose prohibitions do not concern the child in whom he is supposed to be reincarnated.

ANCESTOR WORSHIP.—The cult of ancestors plays as considerable a part in the life of the Ibo of the Asaba district as it does in the case of other tribes of Southern Nigeria. Very commonly the main ceremonies are associated, as at Asaba, with the celebration of the Feast of New Yams. After the death of a man, as soon as his son takes a certain title, he puts the image of his father among the mwǫ, though it may also be placed elsewhere in the house. They also have a spot where they worship their mother.

At g ashi, a son makes a mud image of his father in a corner of the house, and the eldest child offers for his brothers and sisters. This image is put in the ǫgwa, while that of the mother is put inside the house. In some cases the object known as ǫfǫ (Pl. V) is taken to represent the father, cowries are tied round them and the ǫfǫ is put on small heap of mud, either in the house or in the ǫgwa.

In addition to the worship of the immediate ancestors of a man, there is as usual the worship of the ancestors of the ǫbo or idumu. Small houses, the sites of which are commonly seen in the main streets of such towns as Ǫkpanam, serve for this purpose. In addition, in some, if not all towns, there is a cult of umunadi, by which appears to be meant all deceased people of a certain ebo.

Uruci—Vaguely associated with ancestor worship is also an image known as uruči, which is kept both by men and women. In the case of women, uruči appears to be associated with the husband, at any rate at Isele Asaba, and is put by the widow in the house of any brother of her late husband. Where, however, uruči is used by a man, it is said to represent all dead women, and he buries it in order that they may not trouble him. He will then be sure to get a wife. A third statement as to uruči was made to me at O ǫ pa, where the belief seems to be that they represent the dead wives of a man. During his lifetime the husband is said to call them to come and eat and not to trouble the wives who survive.

WITCHES AND SPIRITS.—In this connection may be mentioned also the ajǫmwǫ, or evil spirit, who is a man that has died a violent death. The ajǫmwǫ is said to come and shake the house at night, and when a man shouts no one hears.

In the dry season children are told to come home when the sun is over head, or the ajǫmwǫ will meet them. A sacrifice, usually put in the middle of the street, is offered to the ajǫmwǫ, yams and koko yams are split and with them bored cowries, old bones, fish heads and rags. Sand is taken in the left hand, and the food is cut four times, and the sand added. Then some abobo is taken in the left hand, and the whole is put into a broken vessel which they carry round the house calling on the ajǫmwǫ. If anyone is sick, they come before him and pass the vessel round his head.

At g ashi they say that those who break the law and steal, become ajǫmwǫ, or a man who died a violent death in war and otherwise; but the dead warrior hurts only the man who killed him.

The ajǫmwǫ is often compared to the amosu or witch, who is said to steal young children soon after birth. In Asaba, they have medicine which is said to wake a man when the witch comes. The ingredients are a gag put in the mouth of a man who is going to be killed, leaves on which a head of palm nuts has fallen, the sap of a palm tree, an owl's head and inyi seed. These are parched and seven times seven flies added, and all put in a broken pot at night. They are then put in a long calabash, and hung in front of the house.

A method of dealing with witches is to put a staple in the ground with something heavy on it. This holds the witch, but it must be taken up just before dawn, otherwise the other amosu would come and kill him or her.

The witch is said to kill the victim by taking medicine, and kneeling and calling out the name of the man. A

PLATE VI.

AKBOMALẸGWE AT OGWAŠI. See page 29.

"GATE" OF QUARTER, AND OFFERING FOR ẸRHI, ISẸLE ASABA. See page 19.

common method of dealing with witches is to make them drink sasswood.

Changeling.—In this connection may also be mentioned the belief in changelings. It is said that a child of three years who cannot creep or walk has come through or from a stream. At Ubulubu they take it to the Otọ River with mashed yams on a plate. It changes into a python, and goes back into the stream.

In Asaba the same ceremony is performed in the house, and if the child turns into a snake, it is killed. Some children are said to turn into monkeys. A changeling is known as ṅwa di mwọ, and I have been seriously assured by more than one person that they have actually seen the transformation.

Akbomalegwe.—This fear of vengeance of a slain animal or man is the root of various practices, such as those at the killing of big game, as well as of a portion of the ordinary burial rites.

At Asaba, the head of the slain man was brought to Odogu, who put an eagle's feather on the head of the slayer; the slayer then went to the other olinzẹle (p. 40) to show that he had become omalẹgwe, the slayer of a man or dangerous animal; those who performed this rite plaited palm leaves and put them up before a cotton tree (Plate VI).

At Isele Asaba, when a man went to war and slew another man, he brought the head to Ago and the Onotu;* Ago, Odogu and Iyase put eagle's feathers in his hair. After going round the town for seven days, he brought a cock, meat and drink, and the onotu came and offered the cock to his ikenga (Plate V);† a cotton tree (ak'bo) was then planted in the street. The Onotu came and the head was skinned and buried behind the akbo, and portions of the skin were given to each Onotu and fowls were boiled and eaten.

On the day on which ẹkwẹnsu or ine was celebrated, a man went to his akbo with a cock which he offered and

---

* See p. 40. † See p. 55.

also took one calabash of palm wine not quite full. Odogu then came and took ọbwọdọ and cut the mbubu (calabash) into two; Iyase and Odogu rejoiced over their dead enemies and sang "onye mbu dịyi," "the one I killed is you" (because they do not know his real name). Then they held the matchet and ọbwọdọ in either hand and danced. After this Odogu and Iyase made their own akḃo and mbubu ceremony. The next day logs 4 feet long and 6 inches in diameter were cut and stored in the ogwa between two posts; The log is called nko okbokba; okbokba are properly ebwono and koko yam leaves used for soup; soup was cooked and sprinkled on the logs so that people might not die before the year was out, then the wood was used as fire-wood. A sick person might plant akbo even though he had killed neither man nor beast; if the doctor recommended .him to do so, he paid money and planted the trees ; he might go and ask for the skull of a man killed long before.

HUNTING.—In some respects, the hunter enjoys privileges similar to those which a doctor enjoys. No one, for example, is allowed to seize his property for debt, and the reason given is that the hunter is useful in keeping animals off the farm. This exemption is, however, subject to exceptions in practice, for if a doctor refused to pay a fine on the demand of Okute, his house might be broken down.

As usual, there are special ceremonies when a leopard is killed. At Qkpanam, a messenger is sent to the head chief, and the body put down at the entrance of the ẹbo. The hunter receives an eagle's feather, and offers kola to the mwọ, and the people say "ẹze anẹzu orbi," "the king never steals."

At Onitsha Olona, the customs are much the same, and the hunter is required to dance all night for seven nights. If they kill a bush cat, called onobwo, the forbidden animal of the town, they have to leave it lying, and. the hunter throws one cowry yearly into the bush on the anniversary. This is called " paying the debt of the bush cat." As mentioned under ǫkpalẹbo, the hunter is required to give dues of most animals that he kills to the ǫkpalẹbo.

AGRICULTURAL RITES.—In addition to the ceremony connected with the eating of new yams, various customs are celebrated, which are more connected with the promotion of the growth of yams. At Isele Asaba, four days before the New Yam Feast, two ẹbwo sticks about three inches long, called ifejiǫko ụnǫ, are gathered and taken to the farm, where offerings are made to them. After this they are taken home and kept for the whole year.

At Onitsha Olona, on the other hand, the ẹbwo are kept in the farm and the offerings are made there; and the ifejiǫko ụnǫ is represented by tools used in farming, such as hoe, matchet, etc.

At g ashi the ceremonies are performed in a part of the court near the wives' houses. Here, as elsewhere, the object is to make the yams grow, and they say that this spot chosen to make the heart of the women agree with the farms.

At Obuluku a ceremony known as ẹrba ji aku is performed, the object of which seems to be to call the ẹbwo, which represent the ifejiǫko, from the old farm to the new one. A woman boils koko yams at night and peels them in the morning, adding pepper, salt and oil. In the ǫgwa she stirs it with her middle finger and then kneels on both knees, holding the same finger up. The husband offers the food to the mwǫ and puts some in the woman's hand for her to eat. The rest is offered on the farm and the first and last posts of the irhe (see p. 177) taken out. At the same time the ẹhwo are lifted with a matchet and told to come to the new farm, where one hen is offered to them. After this the old farm is considered to be deserted and the posts used for the yams can be taken for firewood.

MAGIC.—There are a considerable number of magical rites in the Asaba district, the main object of which appears to be to avert evil rather than to bring good; such, for example, is the ceremony known as čuisusu. At Ǫkpanam a doctor is called, and a he-goat and an old basket provided, in which is put a leaf from each house. The goat is tied upon a stick with palm leaves and tutu and an old shield put upon the top with the leaves inside. The men of the ẹbo in order of age fire arrows at the goat, and after the doctor has offered mashed yams the young men take the shield, preceded by the "dividers" of the sacrifice, and run to the place where the post called isusu has to be planted, usually some distance along the road. After planting the isusu, they wash before they return. The object of this is said to be to make the land good and to cause the isusu to leave it. Isusu therefore appears to mean evil.

This rite appears to be performed for the benefit of the whole community. For the benefit of the ẹbo the following ceremony is performed. The doctors come with a basket containing a pig's head. Leaves from the roof of the house are put in the basket, the doctors saying at the same time, "War and fire leave the house." Here, as before, yams, corn and kola are offered to those who perform the ceremony.

Where a girl reaches the age of ten or twelve a ceremony called uke is often performed, which is believed to have the effect of rendering her good and obedient.

At Onitsha Olona, if a man's či has been cursed, the nwago (see Glossary) goes to a doctor at the death of his či. The doctor takes a white ants' nest, unbroken kola and the head of a cock that has not crowed and puts them in a trap. After marking the man's forehead with this medicine, he puts the trap in a tree or forked supports.

A rite of a more positive kind is known as ibe mbubwu. The person who wishes to make it draws a line with his foot in the court of his house. Seven chalk lines are drawn across this and a leaf put on each and the man cuts the leaves in half. The doctor takes up the right-hand halves and the man the left-hand halves. The doctor then takes both in his left hand and passes them down the man's body. He next hands them to the man, who throws them into the bush, and before entering the house draws his right foot along the line drawn by the doctor. This is done by traders to make their trade good, and it is symbolical of breaking down obstacles.

At Ala anyone who wishes to plant cotton must mark his eyes with chalk, so that the cotton will grow well; for cotton itself is chalk, they are the same colour.

Another ceremony is known as onu. At Ibuzọ a hole is dug and the man led before it: a fowl's head is thrown in and various objects passed round his head. All bad spirits and all bad men are called upon to come and eat, and all the objects are put in the hole. The doctor leads the man by the right hand across the hole and says: " Run away "; the hole is then filled in.

Making peace.—War was of frequent occurrence in the old times, consequently methods of making peace were well known. Under ordinary circumstances the ambassadors were the ṅwadiaṇi or ṅwada, that is to say, the children of women who had married from one of the combatant towns into the other.

At Asaba the method of making peace was as follows — Those who had caused the war brought a slave and the other party brought a goat and a cock and a ceremony known as li onini was performed, usually at the boundary. A cotton tree (akbo) was planted over a slave's head; this was the onini and it became a permanent alose. A hole 7 feet deep was dug and the slave put in alive; then the cotton tree, on the first occasion of making peace, was planted on the slave's head and a goat and a fowl sacrificed. On later occasions, when peace had to be made a second time, the price only of a slave would be brought.

At Asaba treaties of alliance as well as treaties of peace were known. The asabwa or obi* was represented by the onoi or rhaza. Each town brought its own alose and the parties swore to do each other no harm, to allow no enemies to pass and to warn each other of the approach of enemies. A treaty of alliance, however, did not mean that they would go

* See p. 38.

and fight as allies in the case of war against a third party, they only supplied guns, powder, etc. If they went beyond this the enemies would never make peace with the town that thus intervened. This ceremony of making alliance was known as ebwando.

At Isele Asaba each party sent money and one slave to the boundary and there the Iyase and Odogu of each town investigated the matter to see who was to blame, the town responsible for the war had to pay the whole; if they did not agree war began again. Ten men with guns stood as guards while the discussion was going on, others hid in the bush but Iyase was sacro-sanct and could not be wounded A slave was buried within a triangle formed by two ẹbwo trees and an ečiči.

At Onitsha Olona the trees planted by the side of the road were ẹbwo and kola on either side and ẹbwe in the middle. Each party brought one goat and offered after a war, and buried the head before the ẹbwe.

At Obuluku to make peace sheep and a goat were provided. The Iyase of each party killed the animals provided by the other and the heads were buried at the boundary and they said, "If anyone causes war again and passes this spot let him die." In addition to these they could also bring alose and the Iyase of each town swore ebwando. The alose were then taken home so that enemies might not come and offer and make the oath of no effect.

At Ezi the ẹbwe tree was planted over the head of a slave at the boundary and each town ate half of a goat sacrificed on the ẹbwe. If after this first peace making war broke out again only kola would be offered to the ẹbwe.

Ebwando.—The ceremony of ebwando might be performed by individuals or sections of a town as well as by two towns. At Onitsha Olona, two men when they made an agreement had to swear on the alose and take kola each from the alose of the other. A man might call his umunna to swear friendship to himself and his household before the mwọ; an idumu might be called before the ani (p. 13) for a similar purpose, or the ẹbo; a man's wife or children might be called upon to make ebwando; all the women of the household of the husband swear to do no magic to cause a wife to be sterile, and the children swear not to give poison.

At Ibuzọ, when two people quarrel in the same ẹbo, the head of the ẹbo calls them and asks them what the cause of the quarrel is; they then eat kola from each other's alose. A man may swear ebwando with his wife also, that she may confess to him any forbidden thing that she does. When two idumu or two ẹbo make ebwando they swear that if they see anything which will injure the other they will tell them; they will not attempt to poison them or put aja for them; if they do the alose is to kill them.

At Obuluku, two idumu meet, each man who has an ọfọ lays it down before the ani, and puts kola on the ọfọ. They swear that if they see anyone stealing or carrying off a woman of the idumu they will not keep silence, and whoever mixes poison for one of the idumu, they will report it, and if they do not, let the alose and the ọfọ kill them.

At Ezi for an iyi umunna the ọkpala brings a staff known as osisi together with ọfọ and pincers. The women of the umunna bring a pepper pounder and the men black-smith's tools. Kola is then put in water in a bowl and these articles washed in the water. The kola is then offered to ani and an oath taken to make no medicine to kill anyone in the umunna.

BURIAL.—It is impossible to give a full account of the burial rites in the Asaba district, for not only does each town, and even each quarter, have its own rites, but these rites, here as else-where, differ according to the rank and sex of the deceased person. In former days for example it was the custom in Ọkpanam to kill a slave when a man holding the title of ẹze was buried. He was dressed up and wore a rain hat upon his head, and carried a fly whisk upon his shoulder. He was tied to the ẹbwo tree which represents ifejiọko (p. 31) and those present fired at him with their guns. He was then washed and buried beneath the ẹbwo.

At the present day at Isele Asaba (Pl. VII) the burial ceremony is as follows :—The body is washed in the part of the house known as ezi obulu, and the corpse is put in a sitting position on a circular box known as mpata. The adẹbo shaves a small portion of his head and another woman completes the shaving. The ada then takes a corn husk and smears chalk in spots all over the body. Thereupon the box of cloth is opened and the body covered with a good mat and wrapped in cloth. When the grave is dug, a calabash is blown to summon the dead man. A goat is sacrificed to the ikẹṅga (see p. 55), which is sometimes split, but if a man has a good son, only a small portion may be taken off it, and the son would take possession of the ikenga. The head of a dog is cut off and the blood dripped in a circle round the corpse. After this a goat is killed " to the feet " and offered, together with fufu. Then kola, roast yam, etc., are offered (Pl. VIII), but the kola is not eaten. One of the pots in which the food is offered is broken. If the corpse is to be buried in a coffin, it is now put in a coffin and taken to the akbo or cotton tree, where a ram is killed. At this point, in former days, a slave would have been put in the grave and the coffin lowered down upon him. When the grave is filled in, the ground is beaten hard and cowries fixed on the surface. A goat is sacrificed and the blood sprinkled upon the grave. Ceremonies of mourning go on for some time, and on the fifth day, the pieces (p. 21), known as nkpụlụči, are cut up and the sons take one piece each. A hen and a he-goat are killed where the dead man washed, and other animals are killed " to cut down ifejiọko and oču̯ču aja." Three months later the idumu of the dead man collect, and yams, a mat, and two pots are brought. The yams are peeled first and the peel pounded in a mortar; a pot is set aside for the peeled yams, and any ọkpala puts fire underneath all shout when the fire blazes. The eldest son of the dead man digs a small hole and the ada sacrifices a hen to it. All the yams are offered and the peeled yams and water are

PLATE VII.

BURIAL : DANCE ROUND THE BODY (ISELE ASABA). See page 36.

BURIAL : MARCH ROUND THE TOWN, CARRYING CORPSE (ISELE ASABA). See page 36.

PLATE VIII.

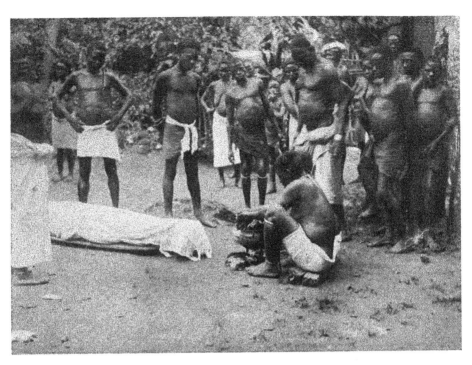

BURIAL: WASHING HANDS BEFORE OFFERING FOOD (ISELE ASABA). See page 36.

ORHAI UKU (GREAT ORHAI) WITH OSŬ (ONIČA OLONA).

poured into the hole. The a d a then takes her mat and one of the pots and says she is going her own way. The children then shave their heads.

The widows have to mourn for three months and remain in the house. They are free on the day on which the ceremony just described above, known as i n i n n i, is performed.

A woman is sometimes taken home to be buried by her own people; sometimes she is buried in her son's house, or on the spot where her son will build a house when he grows up. Where custom requires that a woman should be handed over to her own people for burial, it would be an offence against native law for the husband to undertake the ceremony for himself.

Those who die in infancy are buried under the eaves, children at the edge of the street, and young men and women may, like older people, be buried in the house.

OBI (HEAD CHIEF).—We have already seen under what circumstances the original arrangement as to the head chief at Asaba fell through, so that the office, instead of being held by a man of each ẹbo in turn, was assigned to a particular family. For a time, while Afadie's descendants were still young, a man of another quarter acted as deputy (iẹndo); As soon as Afadie's descendants grew up, however, the regency ceased.

Asabwa and his assessors had to decide cases brought for trial. The dispute was talked over in the umunna, then in the idumu and then in the ẹbo, and the appeal lay to the head chief. In that case the ọkpala of each ẹbo came to the Asabwa's house with the ikeani and the otu rhaza. Asabwa sat on his ukbo or raised seat and informed Iyase of his views as to the case. When Asabwa and Iyase agreed, the assessors retired and took counsel; when all the judges were agreed decision was given, otherwise it was postponed for further consideration. When a case came up about farm land Onoi would speak and two men from each ẹbo were summoned to decide the matter. The witnesses were questioned by any of the court who wished to do so, but there was no oath either for judges or for witnesses. The latter, however, might be called upon to swear upon an alose if there were a conflict of testimony, and oaths might also be taken after the decision was announced, if the parties were not satisfied with it.

Asabwa might receive bribes from law-breakers who wished to gain his assistance, but this did not preclude him from punishing them. The Asabwa received the slaves that were paid by candidates for obu, alo and other titles, but at the present day each ẹbo regulates its own titles.

PLATE IX.

MAN OF ONIĊA OLONA.

CHIEF OF ISELE ASABA.

Asabwa was in some respects the representative of the community. If one man were seized for the fault of another, who was unable to pay to release him, the otu rhaza might collect contributions and hand them to Asabwa who had to deal with the matter. He also received all fines before they were shared out. Asabwa was, as we have already seen, originally compelled to go to Idu in order to claim succession. He took with him two bags, which at that time were worth far more than at present, for 100 cowries would purchase a large goat and 400 a bullock, according to the statements made to me. As, however, my informant added that the price of a slave was two ngugu, I feel some doubts as to his reliability. The candidates paid small sums to the king's messengers at Idu and to the chiefs who led him to the king. The king gave the candidate certain bead ornaments and rubbed chalk on his feet and arms. The ceremonial sword was only given to Qbiọ and Isele. It is said that when the king of Idu died all the people as far as the Niger shaved their beads. One slave was exacted from each town annually and this was paid by the head chiefs.

Among the towns in which the obi occupies an important position may be mentioned g ashi, Obuluku, Onitsha Ubwo and Iseluku. Isele Asaba is an off-shoot of Iseluku and therefore the Ago, as the head chief was called, was less important.

The old men of the town seem to have exercised a certain amount of control over the obi, even in the most important places. At g ashi they said that if the obi violated the law he might be boycotted or even deprived of his position.

In certain towns a woman beyond the control of her husband was handed to the obi, who put her among the ibiale (female slaves) and she virtually became his wife. If she still proved refractory he was at liberty to kill her. This might also be done in the case of a woman who refused to go to her husband. The male slaves corresponding to the ibiale were the ibiagwale, but at any rate at Obuluku they had much more freedom and left the king's service when they married their wives. They would, however, go to a particular quarter known as obwenta.

At Ukunzu the right of succession to the title of obi was so far peculiar that it was .not confined to the direct line. The title might be taken by any of the obi's umunna and the decision appears to have rested with the Onotu.

NZELE.—In several towns in the Asaba district there is a body of men selected in the various ebo to act partly as councillors to the obi or head chief and also to exercise a restraining force upon him, and partly as administrative officers; they are known as nzęle, olinzęle or onotu. In a certain number of cases the offices are hereditary, in others the office bearers are selected either by divination or acclamation; some towns have elective and hereditary dignities. Where the dignities are not hereditary, the selection is usually confined to a particular quarter; it may be limited to each idumu or umunna in turn.

In Asaba, as elsewhere, the dignitary styled Iyase was a highly important functionary. He was the mouthpiece of the town both in judicial cases and in communications with other towns; together with the otu rhaza he had semi-judicial and semi-administrative powers of dealing with law-breakers. If a man who was ordered to leave the town as a punishment for an offence refused to go, the otu rhaza and Iyase might break his house down and hand the man's property to Asabwa.

The leader in war was known as Odogu, and though he did not leave the town, young men who brought heads back, took them to him and put ǫmu (palm leaf) through the mouth or fastened it to the tuft of hair upon the crown. When there was a disturbance with people of another town Odogu had to go to the " end of the street " and then the young men went to war. There is a saying that " Odogu cannot go to a disturbance and do nothing." When anyone was seized he was sent to Odogu to keep, for if he ran it was Odogu's duty to bring him back or seize a substitute; in the absence of her husband, Odogu's wife might be put in charge of a pawn. If a woman refused her husband, Odogu had to deal with the matter.

Onoi carried the ǫfǫ of the whole town. He was one of the elders of the otu rhaza; when a new otu rhaza succeeds, which happens every ten years, ǫmu is planted in the iluku or big street by each man who joins the otu rhaza. A dog is sacrificed and the blood sprinkled on the ǫmu and its body put in the house of the okei rhaza. On the next day they meet in the house of the okei rhaza and divide the dog. The Onoi then takes 1s. 8d., a cock and some palm wine, etc., to the Onoi of the previous rhaza. After counting up to 11 (for the ten years that they serve) he hands the articles he has brought. Onoi is chosen from the first of the four ǫbwǫ who become otu rhaza and a doctor divines from which umunna he shall be taken. If anyone broke the law the Onoi could go to the ǫbo and seize a goat or fowl. If the animal seized was not that of the actual culprit, money might be paid and the animal released ; a man who could not pay the fines could be outlawed. Where a breach of the law occurred a complaint was made to the Onoi, if it was in his own ǫbo, otherwise the complainant would go to Asabwa. It was part of Onoi's duty to sacrifice to all the alose of Asabwa. He went into the street and seized a victim, not as a member of the otu rhaza in this case, for the offender whose deed made the sacrifice necessary was liable to refund the cost of the animal to its owner ; the sacrifice might be postponed till the next big annual sacrifice. When the workers went out Onoi led the way with ǫfǫ.

Another important functionary was Okei Okute, often called simply Okute. He had a body of men associated with him known as iru Okute, slaves of Okute. If anyone, even the Asabwa, committed a forbidden act, it was Okute's duty to reprove him, and he might break down the house of anyone who disregarded constituted authority. If, in a quarrel, a less powerful man feared that his property might be seized, he might put it in charge of Okute. Okute announced new laws; he also stopped the market when the ikei ani had decided that it must be done.

The olinzẹle (dignitaries) at Asaba were as follows: Asabwa, Onirhe, Odafe, Iyase, Isabwa, Osodi, Ozọma, Odogu, Ọmu, Adaisi (?), (Okute), (Onoi).

When we turn to the remainder of the district we find that some of the olinzẹle found in Asaba are found practically everywhere. Each town has a head chief, though those which have been recently founded, like Ubulubu, or those which were barely within, or not within, the sphere of effective Bini influence, have chiefs of only minor importance. Iyase is found in every town, for he is the spokesman of the town; Odogu is found in nearly every town. Ozọma, or Esama (if, indeed, these are identical), are found everywhere, except as Ala and Ibuzọ. Onirhe is found at Asaba, Ọkpanam, Isele Asaba, g ashi, Obuluku, Onitsha Olona, Ukunzu and Nsukwa; but, on the whole, though contiguous towns tend to have the same olinzẹle, there is nothing like the same amount of grouping that we find in the distribution of the systems of titles (see p. 54). It need hardly be pointed out that the influence of Benin City has, obviously, counted for much in the nomenclature, if not the origin of the olinzẹle, Odogu, Iyase, Ozọma and Osodi, are names obviously derived from those in use at Benin City, and this is hardly surprising when we remember that messengers were sent at intervals to Benin City, and that the head chief or his representative visited Benin City to procure the sanction of the king to his succession.

The most important functionary was, undoubtedly, Iyase, for he had to enquire into all breaches of law. At Onitsha Olona, Iyase had to find out the cause of a quarrel between town and town, and to secure the release of any townsmen who had been seized. In cases of murder he acted as a kind of sheriff, and led the onotu to seize the property of the idumu. He was the executioner, or, at any rate, superintended the execution; when an okpala's wife committed adultery, or a woman abused her husband, she was struck by Iyase with his ọfọ, as a sign that she must be sold and quit the town for ever. Where an assault was committed, Iyase called out the onotu, and in a case of accidental homicide he took the gun and the hunter's outfit. He had to deal with cases of suicide, and, generally speaking, all complaints were laid before him and he carried them to the head chief.

At Obuluku, Iyase had control of the young men, for the okwelegwe was only the superintendent of the work. The Iyase was in charge of the building of obi's house; he searched for runaway slaves belonging to obi. In time of drought he went to the bush and searched for a victim to offer to the mwo, but, as a set off, Ozoma, and not Iyase, was properly the spokesman in a meeting.

At Onitsha Ubwo, Iyase controlled all the town, but okwelegwe looked after the roads and streets. Iyase had to see that the contributions in kind provided by candidates for titles, were sufficient.

At Obompa, Iyase controlled all the young men, and when one of the olinzele died he had to assent to the choice of successor, which was announced to him by the four eldest men in the ebo, in whose hands the choice lay. Generally speaking, it lay with Iyase to decide in cases of murder whether the culprit should be hanged or whether compensation was to be received by the family of the murdered man.

At Okpanam some of the functions of the Iyase were carried out by the Ezobu (king of killing). The head of a man killed in war was brought to him first, and if he refused to put chalk and an eagle's feather on the head it was a declaration that the slayer was a murderer. Every three years, about the middle of March, the ceremony of Enaka, or dancing and striking matchets, was held before Ezobu by men who had killed wild beasts or a man.

At Ibuzo Ikwele, who was also found at Okpanam, fulfilled the functions of Ezobu, and it was part of his duty to bury the head of the man who was killed. Although Odogu was the leader in war, his functions required him to stop at home instead of going out with the warriors.

Under ordinary circumstances onotu is synonymous with olinzele. At Okpanam, however, onotu was the name

given to all the young ẹze, who were in the same position as
the otu rhaza at Asaba (see p. 47). At Onitsha Olona the
okwẹlẹgwe occupied a more important position than in
many of the towns, for he was the head of all the ọkpala (see
p. 57), but this appears to have been because he was a sort
of deputy of Onirhe, who appointed him ; Onirhe himself was
the next senior to the head chief. When they killed a goat
as a fine for a breach of the law he offered it to ikẹṅga. In
Onitsha Olona, contrary to the rule stated above, Odogu
could go to the war.

At Ala, as at Onitsha Olona, the head chief is virtually
only one of the olinzẹle, for his position is not hereditary,
he is simply the senior ọkpala or ẹze. He is known as
Obwelani or Onoi.

At Ala the control of the town was in the hands of the
Obwelani (or Onoi) and of the Iyase, who chose some of the
ṅkpalo (p. 54), as a sort of jury where a case was being
tried. After these jurors had consulted and come to a
unanimous decision they announced it to Iyase, who com-
municated it to Obwelani. Bribery alone justified Iyase and
Obwelani in refusing to accept it. Another important
functionary at Ala was Okute; if there was a quarrel about a
palm tree Okute had it in charge till the matter was settled;
when a woman stole yam sticks for firewood the farm was
put in charge of Okute ; he was the executioner in cases of
serious offences. It was laid down that when an ọkpala
summoned a meeting no woman was to come near.

At Ibuzọ, where the head chieftainship was likewise not
hereditary, the chief was selected not by seniority but by age.
Cases were tried before him, the men of the next two ọbwọ
to him, the ọkpala, and possibly several others.

At g ashi, where the dignitary second to obi is called
Onirhe, the son of the dead obi took a slave to Onirhe in
order to receive the title from him.

At Oboluku all the nzẹle were hereditary positions,
though a deputy might be appointed if the eldest son were
young or if the last holder had no son. The olinzẹle, the

ǫkpalebo and the ike ani, that is the old men who had taken ęku title, were the law-makers.

At Idumuje, on the other hand, all the nzęle, with the exception of the obi, were chosen by the town.

EZUBO.—In some of the towns of the Asaba district the young men are organised in what may be termed companies or ǫbwǫ. This system is found in Asaba, Ibuzǫ, Ǫkpanam and Ala. An ǫbwǫ includes all male children born 15 months on either side of a given date, that is to say, no member of an ǫbwǫ is more than $2\frac{1}{2}$ years older than any other member.

At Asaba the ǫbwǫ come in alternately in March and September, and a list has been made tracing the ǫbwǫ back to the year 1796. The compilation was made from information given by men of the Ajaji quarter, and the names given are not necessarily those of the heads of the ǫbwǫ.

ǪBWǪ ALREADY EXTINCT.

	Head of Obwo.		Born.	Ezubo.
1.	Mǫnu	...	Sept., 1796	Onwuanabu of Ǫnaji.
2.	Ama isienu*	...	March, 1799	..
3.	Onianwa	...	1801	..
4.	Okwusǫgu	...	1804	,,
5.	Okonta	...	1806	Utǫmi of Agu.
6.	Obwe	...	1809	..
7.	Enainya	...	1811	
8.	Ebuike	...	1814	,,
9.	Enewe	...	1816	Omękęm of Ajaji.
10.	Ebǫla	...	1819	,,
11.	Aiyagasi	...	1821	
12.	Ǫfǫgu	...	1824	,,

* Last of company and died 1903.

Qbwǫ of which Representatives survived in 1912.

Head of Obwo.			Born.	Ezugbo.
1.	Osadẹbe*	... ...	1826	Nwacie of Uboẹnta.
2.	Isibisi ...	... ...	1829	..
3.	Keri ...	... ...	1831	
4.	Kanẹme	... ...	1833	,,
5.	Rhalim ...	... ...	—	Alalogu of Ezenei.
6.	Kaje ...	... ...	- -	,.
7.	Oṅwuka...	... ...	—	
8.	Nzẹmẹka	... ...	—	,,
9.	Eluemụnǫ	... ...	—	Edeatu of Agu.
10.	Čima ...	... ...	—	..
11.	Idigba ...	... ...	—	,,
12.	Cukuẹdo	... ...	--	,,
13.	Qdiwe ...	... ...	—	Moyo of Qnaji.
14.	Gwanniru	... ...	--	,,
15.	Mǫzia ...	... ...	—	
16.	Čukyra ...	... ...	—	,.
17.	Ṅwadei ...	... ...	—	Ojineka of Uboẹnta.
18.	Iwẹbi ...	... ...	—	..
19.	Aribwǫgu	... ...	—	.
20.	Okwudei	... ...	—	,,
21.	Okobi ...	... ...	—	Okoma of Ajaji.
22.	Qnwǫcei...	... ...	—	..
23.	Okaka ...	... ...	—	
24.	Okuji ...	... ...	—	,,
25.	Okŏlo ...	... ...	—	Okoinye of Agu.
26.	Oru ebu...	... ...	—	,:
27.	Jidowa ...	... ...	—	,,
28.	Anam aga noke		—	,,
29.	Izediono...	... ...	—	Ocei of Ezenei.
30.	Ofili ...	... ...	—	..
31.	Cinyemolo	... ...	—	
32.	Uzo mecina	... ...	—	,,

* In 1912 two of the first and second, four of the third, and ten of the fourth and fifth together survived.

Head of Obwo.			Born.	Ezubo.
33. Ciwetanoma	...	...	—	Odini of Ubwenta.
34. Onyenyozie	...	...	—	..
35. Mosi eli ...	...	...	—	

Every 10 years an ẹzubo is appointed and the names of these ẹzubo are also given.

At the age of about five a boy joins the ọbwọ of his idumu, when he is 10 these ọbwọ are united and become an ọbwọ of the ẹbo, and when he is about 18 the ọbwọ is "called out for work." A man belongs to these ọbwọ, known as otu okwẹlẹgwe, for about 25 years unless he previously takes the ẹze title and is free from work. Every 10 years when a new ezubo is selected, the four top ọbwọ of the otu okwẹlẹgwe become akboluku or elders of the work. The first two remain at home to detect shirkers and the other two go out to direct the work. After ten years the akboluku become the otu rhaza, who are the deputies of the ndičie or otu okwa. At the present time the ndičie appear to belong to nine different ọbwọ, though according to my informant there should be only five. As, however, by reckoning up the old men in each quarter, I discovered that there were two survivors of the ọbwọ born in 1826 onwards, two of the next, four of the next, and ten between the next two, seventeen in all, I am inclined to think that the larger number is probably correct. At any rate the rhaza appear to be a numerous body when they enter on their term of office. On the last occasion there is said to have been a total of 400. As the population of Asaba is only 27,000 this means one man out of every 35 males. The head of all the ọbwọ is the okwẹlẹgwe, usually the head akboluku, but a younger man might be chosen. In each ẹbo an ẹzọbwọ is appointed, but the functions do not seem to be very definite.

When the ezubo is appointed the whole town meets and a doctor divines. The man appointed comes before the last ezubo to get ọfọ; he lives 25 days in a bush house and two boys cook for him; he cannot eat any food which has not been cooked in an ukoni and cannot carry a load on his head. After the period of seclusion the woman who cooks for him must wear a special cloth; in the bush house a fire always has to be burning, and if it goes out special fire has to be fetched from Okwe. If the candidate dies, ashes are put on him but they do not lament for him. After receiving iči marks he goes to "Udo bush" and his head wife washes his back, which she may not do later; then he puts anklets on and rubs camwood all over his body. At new yam time he gets his own New Yam Feast on the day known as afọ ubwo, and the following day he sends the old year back. All the young men take long sticks known as ubolo and dance after the ezubo through the town a dance called iwu. Before he comes out and after he goes home boys of the age of 20 and downwards fight with these sticks on these two .days. There is a saying about this kind of fighting "Ubulo adebu awọ," "a stick does not kill a frog," that is, a quarter staff will not kill anyone. Women follow the dance carrying small switches and they collect money to buy palm wine for the young men. To the feast mentioned above come the ọbwọ and uke, *i.e.*, the ọbwọ next below the one of the ezubo. The ẹze of these two ọbwọ drink palm wine only. As regards the ọbwọ, any member of it is bound in honour to stand up to any other member in wrestling or any other kind of contest, and any member of an ọbwọ who commits adultery with the wife of an ọbwọ mate is fined seven goats. No one may come armed to a meeting of the ọbwọ.

As regards the number of ọbwọ in the other towns mentioned above I recorded 32 at Okpanam, and there appeared to be about 31 at Ala, though here the information was more uncertain. There were 34 at Ibuzọ. Thus in the towns mentioned the oldest men were between 80 and 90, but it is a curious fact that in the Hinterland the number of old men appears to be far smaller. So far as my observation went, there were no men over 80 in most of the towns, though the absence of ọbwọ made it difficult to determine the ages.

At Ala boys become active members of an ọbwọ at the

age of about 10 years. After the New Yam Feast they meet in the house of their head to drink palm wine. They all join in trying to discover a thief ; if a member commits adultery with the wife of another member he is fined. About 10 years after joining the ǫbwǫ a man becomes one of the ibwobwo (men liable to be called out to work) and takes his share in the work of the town. Eight ǫbwǫ do work and one supervises them ; the ǫbwǫ between the ibwobwo and the supervisors are called owai. The work of the owai is to smooth a wall made by the ibwobwo or to straighten bad places. They cut the bush on the side of the farm roads while the ibwobwo clean the grass. They remove trees from the road. The owai subscribe for sacrifices, together with the ikei, but the ibwobwo contribute nothing beyond palm wine. When a slave was dragged to the river in the ceremony of purification the owai officiated ; he was first of all dragged widdershins round the tree which represents ani, and then each quarter, Ukumaga and Oinya excepted, in turn dragged him towards the river. Anyone whom they meet took a leaf and throws it on the slave, saying " alo soi," " may the forbidden thing follow you."

I enquired of a man whether women had any ǫbwǫ and he said, " No, of course not, they have no time to meet or do anything."

At Ibuzǫ each ǫbwǫ has an ęzǫbwǫ for the whole town. Four ǫbwǫ form the workers and after 5 years two more ǫbwǫ come in and take the place of the two top ones ; here, therefore, a man is required to give 10 years. All the ǫbwǫ above the workers are akboluku.

ǪKPALEBO.—An important part in the life of the people is played by the various persons who enjoy the dignities of ǫkpala and ada. These ǫkpala, namely the ǫkpalebo, ǫkpalidumu and ǫkpalumunna, must be carefully distinguished from the holders of the ǫkpala title, which are found only in certain parts of the district.

The ǫkpalębo and his counterpart among the women, the adębo, are selected in various ways. In Asaba, where everyone appears to trace his genealogy back to Nevisi, the founder, the oldest man of the oldest generation is the ǫkpala of the ẹbo, irrespective of the actual age ; that is to say, if a man of 20 in the sixth generation is the oldest survivor of that generation, he takes precedence of a man of 90 in the generation below him, and the same is true of the ada.

At Ǫkpanam, on the other hand, the ǫkpala seems to be the oldest man in the ẹbo. There is, however, a third method of selecting the ǫkpalẹbo which is practised at Isele Asaba and elsewhere, namely, by seniority in rank ; that is to say, that when a new ǫkpala is to succeed, they enquire who took the ǫkpala or other significant title first, and he succeeds as to the title ǫkpalẹbo. This method of selection, of course, does not apply to the ada.

Various fees have to be paid both in the case of ǫkpala and ada, and they also have to offer food to the community. If their means do not permit them to perform all these ceremonies, their kin may assist them ; and if an interval occurs between the death of the last holder of the title and the succession of the new one, one of the family of the last holder acts as deputy (ičẹndo), and may continue to hold the office for years.

The ǫkpalẹbo has a certain amount of responsibility for the maintenance of order in his ẹbo, and is in more than one way the legal representative of the ẹbo. In some places, for example, the trees, which elsewhere are regarded as common property, are said to be vested in him. In other places he takes the property of anyone who dies without a known heir.

In Asaba anyone who buys a slave or a cow puts them in the charge of the ǫkpalidumu, whom they call their father, the object being that no one, in or out of the idumu, may seize for debt the property so entrusted to the ǫkpala, for his property cannot be seized. The work of the ǫkpalẹbo, in addition to the maintenance of order, is largely concerned with the social life of the people, and in particular with breaches of the marriage law. To him falls an important part in the ceremonies which follow the confession of adultery on the part of a wife.

As the representative of the community he receives various services from them. He is virtually the father of the eldest son in each family, and he receives the bride price of the eldest daughter. The remaining members of the community owe him certain dues, some of them annual, some of them payable only under certain circumstances. The hunter, for example, in Asaba, has to render to the ǫkpalębo a certain portion of the meat, and in the case of an animal with a valuable skin, like the leopard, also the skin. Curiously enóugh, at Asaba antelopes are not included among the objects on which the ǫkpalębo has a claim, although by way of bringing up the children in the way they should go, a small brown dove, known as nduli, about the size of a blackbird, is divided into shares, one of which goes to the ǫkpalębo.

The ǫkpalębo is the custodian of the nze, an object, often a box, which represents the founder of the ębo (Plate V).

Much of what has been said about the ǫkpalębo applies also to the adębo, but she has additional functions in that it is her duty to hear the confessions of girls before they go to their husbands, and also of married women who have committed adultery. Over and above this she is charged with annual purificatory ceremonies in the houses of men holding various titles. In consideration of this she receives certain dues from the community. Generally speaking, if a house is regarded as polluted, the ada may be summoned to purify it, which she does by means of one or more fowls, which may be either carried round and released, or beaten upon the ground until they die.

ǪMA.—Under ǫkpalębo have been given details of tribute and other duties owed by all or nearly all persons to certain dignitaries. The ǫkpalamunna, who is the lowest of these grades, is also known as the ǫkpalannа. A man's mother's ǫkpalanna is his ǫkpalanne. Different from these again are the ǫmanna and ǫmanne or ǫma proper. The ǫmanna at Ezi appeared to be the eldest male on the side of the father's mother. Of all these different kinship titles, however, the only two that seem to occupy an important position are the ǫkpalanna and the ǫmanne, inasmuch as dues are rendered to both of them.

Ǫma is the name given at Ibuzǫ to the image of mud which represents a dead mother in the house of her eldest daughter; all the family meet there and offer yams. As soon as a man gets a wife he offers ten yams and one mbannu.

Exactly as dues are offered to the ǫkpalamunna as the sacrificer to the founder of the umunna, so dues are rendered by a family to a person who "has them in ǫma"; and just as a different rule prevails as regards service to the ǫkpalamunna for the first-born of either sex and the other members of the family, so in the case of ǫma. At Isele Asaba the eldest daughter is the ǫma and receives three bags out of the bride price for the eldest daughters of all her brothers.

At Onitsha Olona the eldest daughter, C, of a family serves her maternal grandmother, A, if she is alive, and her younger sisters serve their mother, B, and at the death of their mother their eldest sister, C. C's eldest daughter, D, then serves C, and also her other daughters. At the death of C, D would serve her mother's eldest sister, and so on, the regular rule being that the eldest daughter of a family serves the oldest female maternal relative in the ascending line, while the younger daughters serve their mother or their eldest sister.

At Obuluku I was informed that the ǫma was like an ǫkpala to a woman, but men as well as women are in ǫma. If there are two sisters, A and B, and if A's daughter has two children, C a girl and D a boy, C has D in ǫma. At her death D is in ǫma to B. The ifęnru for ǫma is one leg of duiker, one hen, one vessel of oil, and nine yams, to be sent when the ǫma is going to offer to her mother. One bag is also paid to the ǫma at the marriage of a girl who serves her. On the other hand a man who is in ǫma to her may be helped by her to pay the bride price.

At Idumuje Ụnọ all are in ǫma to the oldest woman of the oldest generation according to my information, but as I not investigate this by means of genealogies it is possibly wrong; for at Idumuje Uboko the ǫ̓ma may be a man or a woman, and is either the mother or the eldest descendant of the mother, but the eldest child of the mother is in ǫma to the mother's brother or sister.

At Onitsha Ubwo the eldest child has his brothers and sisters in ǫma and is himself in ǫma to his mother's sister.

At Ukunzu, where the ǫma custom has probably been introduced in comparatively recent times, there are certain irregularities. In one case that came under my notice a woman was said to be in ǫma to the son of her mother by her second husband, though he was naturally the younger; I think the mother was dead. The eldest son was also in ǫma to his mother's half brother, and had himself all his brothers and sisters in ǫma. Isebwe, the woman in question, had her son's children in ǫma, but they are now dead.

At O ǫ pa the eldest son has the other children of his own mother in ǫma, and is himself in ǫma to the eldest brother of his mother. If the mother's brother dies without sons he then stands in ǫma to his mother's ǫkpalębo. If there are only daughters, the first daughter has the rest in ǫma. A woman brings wood, water, salt, and ogidi to offer; if she has already gone to her husband, cach husband brings five yams and kola, and the woman herself brings five yams.

At Ubulubu, in a case that came under my notice, a man, A, was in ǫma to his mother's younger brother, B, although A himself was not the oldest survivor among his brothers and sisters. B was said to be ǫkpalanne to the mother's children. However, D, the son of C, another brother of the mother, was said to have A's children in ǫma. In another case I found a man in ǫma to his mother's brother, although the latter was the younger of the two.

At Ezi the rules were different again. Men are not owned in ǫma at all. People are in ǫma to their maternal grandmothers or their mothers or their mother's sisters. This was the statement made to me by my informant; in practice I found that men were owned in ǫma and had others in ǫma.

TITLES.—All through the Asaba district it is the custom, as in the Awka district, for a man to attain a social position by certain payments which give him the right to bear certain titles. The contributions in money and kind thus paid by the candidates are divided among those who already hold the title.

The expenditure on titles does not appear to be anything like so great as it is in parts of the Awka district, at any rate, the ǫze title in Asaba appears to cost about £25, and it is only rarely that this amount would be exceeded. There are two well marked geographical groups in the district, corresponding with the distribution of the ǫze title. Asaba, Ibuzǫ, and Ǫkpanam have one set of titles, and the remainder of the district another. Ala, which in other respects is allied to Asaba, was not affected by the tendency to multiply the ǫze title, and falls in line with its neighbours instead of following the Asaba custom.

The first title to be taken at Asaba is that known as ṅkpese; this is a sign that a man is free born; he pays five cows to the head of the quarter, and is thereafter entitled to carry an ivory horn; in olden times, when a man had taken ṅkpese title, one slave was sacrificed at his burial. The next title is known as alo, so called from the ceremonial staff which the bearer of it carries; the holders of the alo title receive a share of the contributions of other candidates; a special kitchen is provided for the holder of the alo and higher titles. Properly speaking, a man can only make alo after his father's death, he is called ṅkpalo.

The third title is that of ǫze, and it has been explained elsewhere how it originated. In making this title a slave was formerly sacrificed. After the completion of the ǫze title, the obu has to be made, which is properly a title confined to those who have killed a man or dangerous beast.

If the ẹze fails to make the obu title in his lifetime, it has to be made, if necessary, after his death. A cotton tree called akbo oḃu is planted in front of his house, and is not cut down until his death.

A man also takes the title of blacksmith (ozo) when a doctor orders. Various payments are necessary for the purchase of the blacksmith's materials. One of the benefits reaped by the ozo member is that no one is allowed to seize any animal belonging to him. A man may also become a doctor (dibia). He beats a drum for seven days and calls the ants, ẹlulu, and the ceremonies are not satisfactory until they have come. A doctor also makes orhai (Pl. VIII), or big medicine, made out of a white ants' nest, which he puts either in the ukoni (kitchen) or in a small house built especially for it. According to the grade attained by the doctor, he is entitled to chalk one or both eyes.

When a doctor gets a patient, a price is agreed upon, to be paid when the cure is completed. The patient, however, is not allowed to observe what remedies a doctor uses, for they will be of no effect. A doctor may also, if a patient does not pay him his dues, recall the sickness by putting the medicine used for the cure into the fire.

At Okpanam dimwọ (p. 11) give the title of ṅkpese to their children or their daughters' children. The title of alo is also known as ẹzẹmwọ, but a man only takes it after his father's death and before that time he has no mwọ of his own. The house is purified, and brooms and mats are removed. During certain parts of the ceremonies, the candidates are secluded, and Nri men are sometimes called in. The influence of the people east of the Niger is seen both here and at Asaba and Ibuzọ in the fact that "going to Udo" is an important part of the ceremonies.

The second class of titles is in some respects more elaborate. It is imposible to give any details of the ceremonies that are performed, but the following is a summary of those found at Isẹle Asaba. A young man gets ikẹṅga izizi, that is to say, he gets his first ikẹṅga (Pl. V) or tutelary image. After procuring the ikẹṅga he washes it and says, "Oǒo pua narụ"; this is apparently a ceremony of purification, but the meaning of "oǒo" is unknown. The ikẹṅga is then fixed in a dish known as abuke with chalk and roots; the arms of the candidate are marked with chalk and they say " Food and money come"; then kola is offered and a cock killed. On the following day twenty cowries are offered to the ikẹṅga, which is put on the ukbo. Food and drink are provided for the ẹbo.

The next title is ẹši or ẹrhi. An ants' nest is got from the bush and taken home, and then put in the bush again near a tree. A doctor goes at night and offers kola at the tree and brings the ants' nest back, drawing at the same time a line of chalk all the way from the tree to the house and saying, "Ẹrhi follow the line of chalk, and come to the house and eat." The ants' nest is put in an old basket for fish, and a tortoise sacrificed to it. The doctor then says, " Let me go home," and receives his fee. The children of the idumu then take ẹrhi, and take it to the place fixed by the doctor, singing "Erhi eat."

The next ceremony is known as orhai. The candidate provides certain roots and an ants' nest, which is put near the wall and covered with medicine so that it cannot be seen. Then the ọkpala of the candidate offers to this orhai, and a dog and other victims are sacrificed on it. The skull is skinned and hung over the orhai and they say the orhai will preserve him; later, a ram is killed with similar ceremonies.

After this a man has his head shaved, leaving a patch in the middle. This is called inyokọnti; he may put a parrot's feather in the patch that is left. A day is fixed on which the candidate dances all night; young men come and build an ọgwa, that is an open front house, for him; he then proceeds to make alo. In the course of this, in addition to various payments, he has to cut ọfọ, put it in a pot and half bury it. The candidate provides himself with ọsisi staves, which are identical with the Edo uxure,* and he next proceeds to find a small girl who will carry his ǫkwači for him.

This girl, known as onye ebuci, is decorated with beads and stays four days in the candidate's house; she does no work for the next three months, and then takes off her beads. Before a girl can become onye ebuči, the ceremony of uke has to be performed for her.

The candidate has now completed his title (ičǫmwo), and is known as ǫkpala. Here, and in most places where an ǫkpala title is taken, the candidate plants an iroko tree in the course of the ceremonies, and fastens a victim, either a cock or a ram, to the top of it. At Onitsha Olona the ram is left hanging to the iroko tree for vultures to eat.

The ǫkpala is, like the ǫze, subject to various ritual prohibitions; if anyone takes his head wife, both man and woman may be killed if they belong to Onitsha Olona, but if the man belongs to another town, war would be the result. Neither ǫkpala nor ǫze may fight with each other, and an ordinary man who fights with an ǫkpala or ǫze incurs a fine. An ordinary man who commits adultery with the wives other than the head wife of an ǫkpala may be fined anything from ten bags to the price of a slave. An ǫkpala who steals may be put to death.

---

* " Report on the Edo-speaking Peoples," Vol. I, p. 37.

IV.—MARRIAGE.

GENERAL.—The ordinary form of marriage in the Asaba district is that in which the wife is purchased by her husband, and resides with him, and the children belong to him (PLI, PLO, PP).* There is also a subsidiary form in which a childless wife purchases for herself, not for her husband, a wife whom she assigns to a "friend," usually chosen by the "wife" herself; this friend takes an oath not to run away with nor injure the woman assigned to him. The relationship thus set up hardly differs technically from a marriage of the ordinary form, inasmuch as the woman is not allowed to change partners at will, and the bond may be lifelong, though in certain localities the death of the "woman husband" (H) results in her "wife" (W) passing to her husband or his heir. A second subsidiary form corresponds to isomi ("Edo Report," vol. I, p. 54); it is known as idebwe.

All over the Asaba district, the ordinary form of marriage usually involves three other stages, though it may happen that the second is omitted, and the first and third coalesce. These stages are (1) the consummation of the marriage, commonly followed by the residence of the wife with her husband for a period up to three months, (2) a period of licence, known as so ṅwaboa, etc., at the girl's father's house, the girl being free to entertain any male friend and cohabit with him; (3) removal to her husband's house and permanent residence with him, after making confession of the names of all her paramours during the period of licence, and absolving the necessary ceremonies of purification, sacrifices and practices ritual commensality with her husband.

---

* Patrilineal, patrilocal, patripotestal.

Up to the time of the consummation of the marriage, the girl should be, and usually is, a virgin, though it may happen that a girl who has reached the age of puberty before a suitor presents himself will take the matter into her own hands and choose a " friend " without her father's knowledge; this is, however, no bar to subsequent marriage either with the friend or another suitor.

Various reasons appear to have facilitated the growth, though they were not necessarily the original cause, of this period of licence. In most places this temporary promiscuity is attractive to the girls, not only as a time of unlimited sexual enjoyment, but also because it involves a respite from household work; their lovers naturally bring presents, and this no doubt is a further inducement; it is worthy of note that in the Asaba district, as on the other side of the Niger, the prevalence of theft is to some extent attributed to the existence of these " friendships."

Elsewhere, at any rate at the present day, the views of the girl appear to be less important; at Ezi, I was informed that the period of licence is intended for the benefit of the mother, who, as well as her daughter, receives presents, though only in kind, from the lovers; the period of licence is here extended to five years, and is not terminated, as elsewhere, by the conception or birth of a child.

To some extent, no doubt, the period of licence must be attributed to the fact that there was little outlet in other directions for the sexual passions of the unmarried men; before marriage, a girl was, and is, carefully kept; adultery with the wives of those who had taken the title of ǫkpala or its equivalent was heavily punished, and though the wife of a young man was fair game so far as native law went, the co-respondent was liable to be assaulted and even killed by the husband on whose rights he had trespassed.

In the present day, the introduction of " white man's " law with regard to adultery appears to have resulted in a great relaxation of morality among the wives of the older men (ǫkpala, etc.), and with this additional safety valve, the demands of the young men upon the young girls should be correspondingly less.

In Asaba and certain other areas, the punishment for adultery with certain women was considerably heavier than elsewhere. The wife of an ẹze or any girl in whose head an eagle's feather had been put was known as isi mwọ; an isi mwọ who commited adultery, was put to death in the olden time. Later, as a concession to humanitarianism, she was allowed to live but expelled from the town, death being the penalty for return : she might re-marry elsewhere, but the original husband claimed no money.

In the present day this custom of expulsion has fallen into desuetude, in some places owing to the guilty parties putting themselves under the protection of a mission, with or without being converted to Christianity.

MARRIAGE CUSTOMS.—The ordinary form of marriage corresponds to the amoia marriage of the Edo-speaking peoples ("Report," vol. I, p. 54). There is, however, a form of sexual relation closely resembling the isomi marriage.

It may be recalled that the isomi wife does not become the absolute property of her husband, though he pays the usual bride price for her; on the contrary she can go to her own family at will, and her children, with certain exceptions, return to her family and inherit property from her brothers.

In the Ibo (and Išan) area the isomi wife, known as idẹbwe, is not paid for and does not leave her father's house, at any rate permanently; a girl is usually left as idẹbwe because the father has no son; she is reckoned as a man, her son, if any, is the heir; if she bears no child she may be joint heir with her father's brother, or may marry a "wife" (W) whose children will inherit.

The idẹbwe is assigned to a friend in the same way as the wife purchased by a woman, and the same oaths are taken to ensure that the "friend" does not abuse his position.

From the point of view of the man to whom the wife is assigned, the kind of marriage in which the woman is purchased by a childless wife resembles isomi marriage, inasmuch as, though she is assigned to a friend, property in his children is retained by the family to which she belongs (after purchase).

Bride price.—A girl is often asked for in marriage the day after she is born, the suitor bringing wood and throwing it down before the mother's door. Some months may elapse before he is finally accepted, but as soon as he is recognised and presented to the umunna (sept, or extended family) he is called upon (*a*) to work on his prospective father-in-law's farm or elsewhere if he needs assistance in clearing the land, planting yams, re-roofing the house and so on, and (*b*) to bring "ifẹnru," gifts of yams, palm wine, cowries, palm oil, etc., on certain ceremonial occasions; he will also give 15 or 20 yams to his mother-in-law once or twice a year besides bringing her palm nuts, wood, etc., and providing for her in his farm a plot in which she plants if'ubwo, vegetables such as pepper, tomatoes, beans, etc., for him to tend.

It is almost universal to repay only the bride price, so that the suitor after rendering services and ifẹnru for fifteen years, finds himself no better off than if he had thrown his yams into the street for his neighbours' goats to eat; he has in fact made a present of perhaps £15 or more to his girl's parents; and if by insisting on her coming to him before she feels disposed he loses his wife, all he receives is the actual bride price, plus if'ọna ("brass" money) and similar out-of-pocket payments. In other words, perhaps three-fourths of his outlay has been thrown away. Unless he can find a girl who has refused her suitor or one who, for some reason, has no suitor, his only resource is to begin again at the beginning and serve fifteen years for another bride. It may be mentioned that it is usually more costly to engage an adult bride, so that the bride price recovered from the parents by a girl engaged in infancy will not be sufficient to bring a wife to his door.

At present the period of licence is merely an episode in the life of a woman; there is, however, a tendency, notably at Oboluku, to transform it into a permanent condition. There it was reported to me that some women after going to live permanently with their husbands had again returned to their fathers' houses and were living as prostitutes, finding such a life easier than the burdensome state of the married woman.

I could not discover any precise number at Oboluku; in a town of 20,000 inhabitants it was impossible to get at the facts in any simple way; I was, however, informed that the cases were numerous. Legislation would undoubtedly be welcomed and it would doubtless be possible to deal with the period of licence and habitual prostitution by one and the same law.

At Asaba the bride price is about £7, but £3 10s. has to be spent on provision of food, probably for the marriage ceremony, and some pounds for ornaments, cloth, etc., for the girl. In addition to this a number of yams are rendered at certain times of the year such as Iwaji (New Yam Festival), the quantity depending upon the age of the girl. When the girl goes to reside with her husband, the girls of her own quarter go and cut wood for her and take it to her husband's house so that she need not fetch wood for some time. She is, however, obliged to share this wood with the other married women of her husband's quarter. When she reaches her husband's house the new wife cooks both for the children and for the older people of the quarter. This is called isinni ụnọ, the beginning of cooking.

An eagle's feather is put on the head of the first wife, who is called anase. This a husband can only do if he has taken alo title. If his wife runs away his title is lost, and consequently it is the custom to take an Asaba wife. If the man is poor and cannot get another wife he makes the people of his own wife swear to return her if she runs. If a man cannot get an anase he takes a bambu pole and carries it to market, and it represents his anase; he puts feathers on it and keeps it; when he gets a wife he can make her anase.

In the case of certain women it is laid down by the doctor that they either must be or must not be anase. In the former case if a man already has an anase the second wife will purchase the title from the first. In the latter case it is possible for the man to make his alo title without putting a feather on her head.

When a man gets a head wife she takes one hen to make ọmụnọ* in the woman's house. This is represented by mud which is rubbed with chalk. A hen is taken to the ukoni (kitchen) and killed there and three akukwa (pot rests) are made. If her husband dies she must lie down beside the corpse with her feet beside his head, a position which is ordinarily forbidden. The work of the head wife is to cook on feast days and on every eke day. She sacrifices on behalf of a man who has taken ẹze title when he is on a journey and may sit on his ukbo or raised seat. If there are quarrels among the other wives she can summon them before her and try the case.

The marriage customs of Asaba have undergone considerable changes in the last twenty years, because in olden time the mere putting of an eagle's feather in a woman's hair bound her legally to the man who did it, whether she was unmarried or a widow. This has now been abolished and in the case of a widow the new husband has to take the woman to her people. He formerly paid 5 ngugu to the ọkpala of her umunna. If a man is paying price for a girl but has not yet married her, the head wife is the one for whom he is paying the price.

At Ọkpanam, as in many other places, a go-between, one of the umunna of the father, conducts the suitor to the house of the father and any complaints about the conduct of the suitor subsequently would be made to this go-between. On the first day the father's consent is asked and the father, mother and go-between discuss the matter. Palm wine is brought and as soon as a man has been presented to the umunna as suitor his position is established. All these preliminaries can be carried out as soon as the child is born, and a man of speculative tendencies may take steps even before the child is born.

As soon as the girl is six or eight she will be consulted and if she declares that she does not like her suitor her father will wait until she makes her choice, and will repay the first suitor from the monies handed over by the second suitor. The Ọkpanam price is seven bags for a girl engaged as a child

---

* Image of her mother (?).

together with one cow valued at ten bags. The former sum is known as ifoji, the latter as oziza.

At Isele Asaba the first step is to throw down wood before the door of the child's mother. This is the common custom throughout the district. After this he approaches the father and mother and they are compelled to consult the father's elder brother. After palm wine has been drunk by the umunna the son-in-law is accepted and told by his father-in-law what he has to do ; he may be called upon, for example, to give a goat to one or more of the umunna. When the girl reaches the age of puberty the father-in-law calls upon the son-in-law to bring ten bags known as elili efi ; he also pays a cow ; five bags go to the mother, the rest to the father or his heir. If the mother is dead, the eldest of her own sisters gets the five bags, failing the sisters her own mother, failing her own mother her mother's sister or the oldest woman in that line (see p. 51.)

When the suitor makes ikęṅga for the girl she receives from him a goat, 100 yams and three bags for the purchase of fish and meat. For beads, cloth and cowry armlets she gets three bags. All these she receives before she goes to her husband. The girl is sent with four conductors to her husband's house. They receive a small payment from the husband and then return home. After remaining two nights in the husband's house she goes home to her father at daybreak on the second day taking with her five ngugu, seven yams and the leg of an animal.

The son-in-law has to make the following annual payments in addition to the single payment mentioned above. When his father-in-law sacrifices to his ancestors his son-in-law brings palm nuts, seven yams and one pot of palm wine. He and his umunna are required to work on the farm of the father-in-law in return for food, soup, palm wine, tobacco and kola. They help to build the father-in-law's house and the umunna tread the mud for it and make the floor. The actual building of the roof is done by the idumu of the father-in-law, though the son-in-law comes to help but without his umunna.

The mother-in-law receives five yams when she has given consent to the marriage; thirty yams at New Yam time, two ntoto when the yams are tied in irhe and one ntoto of ji abana (p. 177). One ntoto is given at the same time to the girl. If other women go with her to the farm two yams may be given to each and the mother-in-law also receives twenty nganaji (seed yams). She further receives seven heads of palm nuts and as many heads of corn as the son-in-law can carry. If the girl refuses to marry the suitor they repay in addition to the actual out-of-pocket expenses ten bags as the commuted value of the yams.

It has been mentioned above that a good deal of value is laid upon the virginity of the bride in the Asaba district. If the husband finds that the girl for whom he has been paying the price has had friends previously to her going to his house he indicates it by marking the yams and the fish which are sent to the parents when the girl returns to their house. After this a girl, who has committed herself in this way, is liable to have her offence thrown in her face not only by her husband but also by other wives when they quarrel with her.

Isele Asaba is so far peculiar in its marriage customs that marriage within the ẹbo is permitted. Originally the two main ẹbo came from Isẹl'uku, where they formed an exogamous unit. Scarcity of wives then compelled them to offer a sacrifice and divide the two ẹbo so that they could intermarry. In Obwoto marriage within the idumu is also permitted because some of them did not come from Isẹl'uku.

It is forbidden to marry in the mother's family. If a distant relationship is traceable, for instance as between son's son's child and daughter's daughter's child, the idumu may go to the okei and offer a goat to the mwọ to be eaten by the ikeẹbo, to "stop the parties from being related." The man and woman themselves may not eat.

At Onitsha Olona a certain amount of work is required from the suitor before the father definitely assigns the child, who may be five or six years old before anything final is done. When this has taken place the suitor has to bring five yams, sixty kola, etc. for his father-in-law to sacrifice to his ancestors. The following day the suitor takes his umunna to thank the father-in-law, who on his side call the umunna to see the suitor. The ǫkpalębo comes and offers kola and touches the foreheads of the girl and of her suitor as they kneel before him. After this palm wine is drunk and the son-in-law visits the members of his father-in-law's umunna singly with his umunna to salute them. The price of the bride is not fixed definitely but varies from three to six bags for the father-in-law; the mother-in-law gets one bag, the ǫkpalębo one bag, the young men of the umunna one bag, the go-between one bag and ten ńgugu to the mother's ǫkpala, that is her eldest sister. After the suitor has made ikęńga for the girl the husband buys cloth and two goats and the girl returns to his house with him. If both belong to Onitsha Olona she goes alone, if to another town young men and girls of her umunna accompany her; they stay three days and are fed by the husband. In the case of a marriage where the girl belongs to Onitsha Olona she returns, with her husband, to her parents at dawn the day after marriage. Five yams are given to the mother-in-law and seven ǫko and palm wine to the father-in-law, but if the bride is not a virgin this payment is reduced. This is the rule where the girl is engaged in childhood.

Where the girl is already marriageable before the suitor presents himself the price may be twenty or thirty bags or even forty if the suitor is from another town. Three bags go to the mother, one to the eldest son, one to the ǫkpalębo and one to the woman who has the mother in ǫma. After this the son-in-law is instructed to bring yams, kola, etc., for the sacrifice to the mwǫ, which takes place on the following day. The son-in-law brings his umunna and a few people from each idumu and the father-in-law's ębo will also come. Where a girl has been engaged under these circumstances she does not return to her father's house after marriage.

At Ala not only the father, but the father's umunna and the mother's brother can call upon the suitor to do work for them. He is also called upon to continue the ifęnru or

PLATE X.

OMOKA. WOMAN OF SOUTH-WEST AREA.

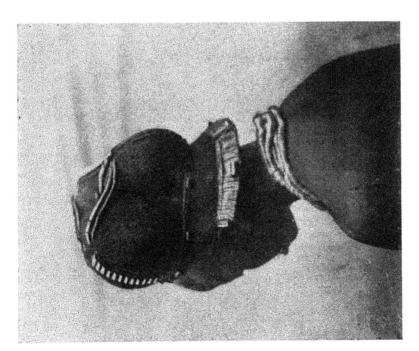

WOMAN OF ISELE ASABA WITH EKWA ALỌ HAIR ;
ỌGALA Ọ'BOBO (PLAIT IN FRONT).

gifts of yams, etc., due before marriage from the time that she has borne her first child until her death. The payments are as follows: three bags to the father, one bag to the mother, one bag to the eldest son, 1s. to the mother's eldest brother or sister, 1s. to the father's umunna. It is not quite clear whether she goes alone to her husband's house; according to one informant the suitor fetches the girl home, according to another she has conductors who carry her ǫkwaci (see p. 17) which she puts in orhai (see p. 22) till she gets her own house, when she takes it before eši (p. 22), an image of mud near the wall. The morning after she has gone to her husband she returns to her parents about 4 a.m. Five days later her husband takes five ngugu, ten yams and a calabash of pahn nuts to her mother and this payment is annually made if the girl is a virgin. She returns to her husband's house after she bears her first child and her idumu will conduct her, carrying the pots and other household articles which are usually purchased by the girl's mother and also yams and fish go to her father.

Under ordinary circumstances, if a girl's mother is dead, one of her mother's sisters may bring her up, but in Ala she may go to live with her suitor's mother. The payment which is ordinarily made to her mother's sister, as a recompense for bringing her up, is, however, made just the same. The Ala customs are different in several respects from those of the rest of the district. Both at Ala and Ebu, if a woman is driven away by her husband and he refuses to build a house for her, she can take all her children to her own umunna, but her husband's refusal must be given in the presence of the umunna of both sides. Where the husband refuses, the umunna cannot accept the responsibility of retaining the children. The ǫkpala of the woman's umunna takes them as his own.

If no children are born, a husband can apply to his elder brother to assign his wife to a friend who swears not to take her as his wife and to allow any children to be handed over to the husband.

The ẹbo is not the exogamous unit in Ala, but this is due to the fact that almost every quarter is made up partly of immigrants from Ida and elsewhere, and partly of those who claim to be natives. These two groups are distinguished as Azanamwọ and Umuẹze and apparently form the exogamous units in the ẹbo.

The ordinary rule is that if a widow marries outside her ẹbo the price has to be paid.

At Ibuzọ the age of a child, when application is made for her, is said to be about 6 or 8. The following are the payments: seven bags as ifọji to the father, who gives three to the mother, twenty five bags as oziza, one bag to the umunua, 1s. to the woman who has the mother in ọma together with ten yams, a fowl, etc., for sacrifice to the oma. If a girl refuses her husband, in addition to the out-of-pocket expenses the ji ogige, 100 yams given annually valued at 5s., are repaid. It is a somewhat curious circumstance that all payments either in kind or in money are made before witnesses even when they cannot be demanded back if the girl refuses to marry.

In most of the district the rule is that when a girl has gone to her husband and returned to her parents, she is required to return to her husband either at the end of twelve months or after a child is born. At Ibuzọ the former rule prevails but she may remain with her parents after the birth of a child, in which case the husband must send food for her to her father's house. While she is living in her parents' house she may go to see her husband and remain not more than one night; if she stays longer she must stay altogether. She is allowed to have friends out of any ẹbo except her own, but the husband's idumu is also excepted. Her friends may come to her father's house when her husband is not there and will also do work for her parents.

At g ashi the rule is for the girl to stay seven months with her husband before she goes back to her parents, and if conception has taken place she remains with him permanently. If she goes back to her father she remains at most three years ; here not only her own ẹbo but all her husband's ẹbo are ruled out as friends. The ordinary rule at g ashi with regard to widows is that the father's brother takes the mother of the eldest son and the eldest son takes the remainder. If, however, a boy is small, the father's brother takes all who have gone to their husband. The girl, however, who has gone to her husband and returned to her father's house may elect to remain in her father's house, or go to the brother of the dead man. As regards marriage prohibitions, it is forbidden to marry in one's own or one's mother's ẹbo or one's father's mother's ẹbo. Marriage in the mother's mother's ẹbo is permitted, but it must be outside her idumu. Such marriages would, however, be rare, for my informants had not heard of any cases.

At Oboluku a girl stays three months with her husband and then returns to her parents, whether conception has taken place or not. After going to her father's house she may stay away three years or return earlier at will. I was informed that in a number of cases girls who had finally gone to their husbands decided to leave them again and return to a small house which they built near their father's house, this after repaying the price. Where a woman does this, the children belong to her father for she is reckoned as idẹbwe.

At Obolonọ a girl goes to her husband for from one to three months or may remain with him altogether. If she returns to her father's house she may remain away as much as three years. This period appears to be growing longer, and here as elsewhere the natives say that formerly a girl's mother sent her to her husband, but at the present day the girl threatens to summon her husband to receive repayment of bride price if any pressure is put upon her.

At Idumuje Uboko application is made for a girl soon after birth, but decision is apparently delayed for some years. When a father-in-law accepts a suitor the latter brings various articles for sacrifice, and the forehead and chest of suitor and girl are touched with kola, which is then offered to the mwọ. When a girl goes to her husband she stays from three to five months and then returns to her parents, where she remains till she has borne a child or at most for two years. If she is the wife of a man who has taken ǫkpala title, here as elsewhere she is not allowed to have friends, but in recent years this custom has probably been broken down, and to this is due, no doubt, the fact that the older men are without exception opposed to the period of licence which follows the return of the girl to her father's house.

Under ordinary circumstances the method of recovering a runaway wife was to seize people connected with her in some way, even though the relationship was no nearer than membership of the same ębo. At Idumuje it was also the custom to apply to the owner of the alose Nęmonica. It was believed that if after this the offending man failed to restore the woman, Nęmonica would kill him. His property had to be brought together with an offering and put before the alose; the valuables were taken and added to the offering, and the rest of the property sprinkled with odo and chalk; the worthless articles might then be removed by the umunna of the dead man.

At Idumuje Ųnǫ, if a man seduces a girl the father can compel him to pay a higher price than usual and at the same time retain the child, if one is born. The child, however, at the age of 10 might go to see its mother and refuse to return. If it showed its wishes in this way it might be purchased at the price of twelve bags.

If a suitor is paying price at the time the girl is seduced he takes the child, and the father may send the girl to her husband at once. The husband pays full price but gives no goat, etc., for the purchase of cloth, and the mother sends no household articles with the girl.

At Onitsha Ubwo a man asks for a girl as his wife the day after she is born by throwing a piece of wood on the ground before the house. The next day he brings a calabash of palm wine, and if more than one man presents himself the one from whom the palm wine is taken is the favoured suitor. The day after this five heads of palm nuts are brought to the mother, who must agree in the choice of the suitor. The head of the umunna is not told until later, but he has only a very limited right of refusal, apparently only if he has a quarrel with the suitor, which will probably be appeased with a few yams and some palm wine. After this offerings are brought for sacrifice to the mwọ, and kola is offered in the usual way. The man is now the legal son-in-law, and is bound to give palm wine to various members of the umunna, ten in all.

The following are the annual ifẹnru. At the sacrifice to the ancestors the mother-in-law receives five heads of palm nuts and a leg of meat; at the sacrifice to ọma 120 cowries, three yams, and a leg of meat; at the igwe dance, seven yams and a leg of meat; twenty yams are given to her when the suitor begins to dig his yams. If the father of the girl is an ọkpala, one yam and meat without bone are sent to the mother-in-law when the father-in-law goes into nzu (see p. 15); when the yams are tied, twenty yams are given to her as "ji ogige" and three yams to each of the two women who help to carry them; at Ifejiọko a leg of meat goes to the mother-in-law; the father-in-law receives five large yams and a calabash of palm wine, which he offers to his ikẹnga; seven yams, a leg of meat, and a calabash of palm wine whenever he entertains a stranger; five yams, four kola, a large calabash of palm wine, and 180 cowries when he sacrifices to his ancestors; a log of wood and a calabash of palm wine when he goes into nzu; five yams at iwaji; five yams and a calabash of palm wine at igwe. These payments go on as long as the girl lives, unless she refuses her husband. The ifẹnru are reckoned in repayment of bride price but not the work. They were formerly reckoned at ten bags. Some people send their daughters to the suitor before the price is paid; this gives him time for collecting money; in this case she stays permanently with her husband.

At Ukunzu the customs are apparently slightly different, but how far this is due to difference of race I was unable to ascertain. The suitor, when the girl is marriageable, may either take her home to his own house or go to her father's house. In the latter case he will take her home the next day. The girl remains with him three months, but it is not uncommon for men to keep their wives permanently.

At Ezi a girl normally goes to her husband after the birth of her first child, but if no child is born she may stay away five years, and I was informed that some wives bear three children before they finally go to their husbands. Apparently it is impossible for a girl to go to her husband and remain with him from the first, and my informants gave as a reason that the mother would be deprived of the profit she derives from her daughter's friendships in the way of palm nuts, yams, etc.

At Nsukwa the marriage customs are widely different from those of the greater part of the rest of the district, for when a girl has gone to her husband she remains with him. Previous to this she may have had friendships with other men, but risks her suitor's annoyance in this case. She is forced to take her suitor whether she likes him or not, and my informants said that this was the rule at Ejema, Ogidi, Esago, Umute, and other places. Where they marry a woman of a town where the custom is different, they follow their own custom, and not uncommonly the Nsukwa woman who marries, for example, at g ashi, remains permanently with her husband.

Confession.—Before, or as soon as, a girl returns to her husband's house, she has to make confession, usually to the adǫbo, of the names of all the lovers she has had. At Onitsha Olona the adǫbo takes ǫfǫ, the girl names her lovers in succession and puts a grain of corn before ǫfǫ at each name, and as she does so she occasionally includes, out of revenge, the name of a man who has offended her. When these proceedings are finished the ada takes a grain of corn and gives a grain to each lover who has been mentioned, who is thereupon obliged to bring a cock and a goat, which are sacrificed to the ǫfǫ. Thereupon all the lovers eat kola, and after this they may meet the girl in the same house. If this ceremony is not performed a chicken must be offered to purify the woman if she meets them, and she is not allowed to suckle a child till she has been cleansed. The girl and her husband then go to the ǫkpalumunna, koko yams are boiled, the ǫkpalumunna entwines his fingers with those of the woman, holding the palms úp, and puts slices of koko yam on the hand of each. The woman takes the slice from the hand of the ǫkpalumunna and the ǫkpalumunna from her hand. She kneels to the ǫkpalumunna and shouts as she rises; the husband eats nothing. The same ceremony is performed where a married woman commits adultery.

At Ala a girl makes confession in the seventh month of pregnancy. A he-goat is required to cleanse her if she has had lovers, otherwise a chicken suffices. A she-goat is sent to the ǫkpalębo of her husband, to offer to nze, after she has borne a child. The girl takes one leg tò her father's house and cooks the rest for the ębo, but the husband does not attend the feast. The one leg is cooked the next day in her husband's house and husband and wife eat together.

In addition to this ceremony the husband may lie in wait for any lover of his wife and pursue him to the boundary of his own ębo. The lover would then take 180 cowries and palm wine to the ǫkpala of the husband to make peace. This, however, is only in the case of a girl who has not yet gone to her husband. Where it is a question of a married woman, the normal procedure is for the ńkpalo (p. 54) to go and kill five or six goats and fine the co-respondent five or seven bags.

At Ibuzǫ, where a married woman commits adultery there is no fine for the man if he belongs to another ębo. The woman brings two fowls and two goats. The goats are offered by the husband to the ndičie and the nze, and he also kills a cock to ada's ǫfǫ. The adębo kills the fowls to nwada. Where the parties belong to the same idumu, a goat is brought to the house of the ǫkpalębo and killed by him. The meat goes to the men and women of the quarter, but the wife herself gets the head of the second goat which is killed by the husband. Both goats are provided by the co-respondent. The husband brings yams and meat to the house of the ǫkpalẹbo, and they eat together in his house.

At Ogwashi, before a girl goes to her husband, she confesses to adẹbo and takes with her a hen, fish, and yams. The ada kills the fowl to the calabash where ǫfǫ is kept. The girl cooks, the ada gives food to husband and wife in their clasped hands. The cloth of the girl is changed and hung in the street in which the cult of ancestors is kept up.

In the case of a married woman, if the husband had taken a title, the co-respondent was redeemed with one cow or sold. Adultery with the wife of a young man is a minor matter and the fine is a goat, a cock, a hen, and a new cloth. In both cases the ceremonial meal in the house of the ǫkpalẹbo is obligatory.

At Oboluku the girl makes confession in her husband's house and may be cleansed with a chicken. After this she is bound to be faithful to her husband even if, as sometimes happens, he sends her back to her father's house to bear a child because he has not completed payment of the bride price. In the case of a married woman, the co-respondent used to be fined about £5, which was divided between the ǫmu, the obi, and the olinzẹle and ikei ani, three portions in all. The husband received money out of this to buy a goat and perform the other ceremonies, for which a chicken, a hen, a cock, a goat, and three pieces of cloth were required. The wife was then sent to the obi and, unless she belonged to the same ẹbo, became his wife. If she belonged to the same ẹbo, she might be sent away to a distant place to another husband. At the present day they complain that women who are unfaithful to their husbands say, " You cannot send me to the obi now, what can you do to me ? "

At Idumuje Uboko, when a girl goes to her husband, all the eldest daughters of her husband's ẹbo assemble. The girl gives corn to the adẹbo and two piles of the grain are made, according to whether a lover has been accepted by the girl or whether she has refused him after he has made advances. The girl then brings a goat and a cock and changes her cloth. Animals are sacrificed to ọfọ by the adẹbo, and the girl and her husband are purified with two chickens. Husband and wife then go to the ọkpala and eat part of the food after the ọkpala has offered to the mwọ. The girl is accounted as a wife from the day that she has made confession.

Adultery with the wife of obi was punished by hanging the co-respondent or selling him into slavery. At the present day, if the woman is the wife of an ọkpala the fine is £5, and the ceremony of purification has to be performed " for the ground." The woman may be sent to obi as a wife. In some cases the women of the quarter, both here and elsewhere, inflict their own punishment on an unfaithful wife. I was told that at Idumuje Uboko the recognised procedure is to rub the woman with yam juice and then rub in pepper. The husband might also attack the co-respondent with a matchet.

At Idumuje Ụnọ, when a girl goes to her husband, the mother brings a goat for her daughter and the husband offers the goat to nze. The girl then cooks after making confession to ada, and husband and wife eat from each other's linked hands. If after this a man solicits her, the umunna sends a message to him and the man brings cloth, a goat, two chickens, and a cock; the ọkpalẹbo offers the goat to ọfọ and the ada offers the cock to her ọfọ. The head, liver, and heart of the goat are cooked in soup, and husband and wife eat from each other's linked hands. The elders eat the rest of the liver and heart. The ọkpalẹbo takes one ear and the jaw, the ribs go to the young men, two legs to the husband, one leg to the ọkpalẹbo and one leg to the elders. A portion of the head seems to go to the young men and the rest to the husband. One wing of the cock is given to the elders by the ọga or divider, and the husband gives a wing to the adẹbo and takes one leg himself.

At Onitsha Ubwo the punishment for adultery on the part of a married woman depends upon the status of her husband. A young man fights the co-respondent, but if he uses a matchet he would be fined four goats according to the usual practice; afterwards the co-respondent sends 1s. to the husband to make peace and they eat kola together. If the husband has taken ǫkpala title he notifies the ǫkpala members; they collect and inflict a fine of three bags, together with five ngugu, to the ǫga, and ten ngugu to "take up the seat of the elders of the ǫkpala." The husband's ada then obtains a cock, a goat, and a chicken from the co-respondent, and hears the confession of the woman. The ada purifies the wife with a chicken and kills the goat and the cock to her ǫfǫ; the ǫkpalębo then gives kola to the husband and wife.

At Ukunzu the girl goes to her husband before confession and the adębo comes and calls her out; after confession, the men whose names have been mentioned have to provide a goat, a hen, and three chickens, the latter to purify the husband, the wife, and the house. The hen is sacrificed on the ǫfǫ ada, and the ada changes the woman's cloth and keeps the old one. The ǫkpalębo sacrifices the goat before the mwǫ, and offers kola to them. The woman receives some of the kola from him and the husband himself from the ada. The ǫkpalębo cuts food for the woman and the ada for the man. If this ceremony were not duly performed the woman would have to confess again. In the case of a married woman the purificatory ceremonies are described above. The punishment for the woman is as follows. She is called by ada and a hairy seed called abwala is rubbed all over her body. Her head is shaved and a drum put on her back; filth of various kinds is rubbed over her and rags put on her; then she starts from her husband's house and the drum is beaten and the woman keeps shouting her own name with the words "Alo kai ęme," "the abomination I have done."

At Obǫmpa the adębo hears confession in her own house,

and the ǫkpalẹbo and the woman eat kola from each other's hands. Where a married woman, the wife of an ǫkpala, commits adultery the obi causes the "ozi" drum to be beaten and a fine of ten bags is inflicted.

At Ubulubu the ceremony in the case of a girl going to her husband does not differ essentially from that already described. In the case of a married woman the adẹbo calls for the woman and takes the offending wife to a tree called oko; she is tied to this and abwala seed rubbed on her neck. They then flog her home, saying, "You want to kill your husband," and seize all her household goods; the woman has to pay a fine of one goat to the ǫmu. After this the ada takes her home and hears her confession; the woman has to draw a chicken tied with a palm leaf round her house and mash odo and sprinkle it. A hole is dug where she makes confession and corn put in. Blood is run into the hole and meat eaten outside the house and then the bones are buried in the hole. After this the usual ceremonial meal has to be taken in the house of the ǫkpalẹbo.

At Ezi a girl makes confession to the ada umunna, and each accepted lover has to pay sixty cowries and join in providing a goat and a cock which are offered in the first wife's kitchen. The unmarried girls of the husband's umunna eat the meat. The girl's mother brings a cock and fish to purify the body of the husband, and when these are roasted, small boys eat them. The ada "washes" the husband's mouth with mashed odo leaves and his tongue with an egg, which he throws in the middle of the street. The following day the girl cooks in the head wife's house and brings the food before the ǫgwa, where the ada puts it in the linked right hands of man and wife. Each portion of food is then transferred to the hand of the other party and husband and wife eat. After this no co-respondent is to stop and chat with the woman or say to her: "Ainyai di ṅwa," "your eye is like this." For doing so he may be fined three bags and a goat, none of which, however, would go to the husband, for the money is considered to be defiled.

In the case of a married woman the fine for the co-respondent varies from five to seven bags and from two to seven goats, together with victims for sacrifice. No penalty is known for adultery with a wife of one of the olinẓele, for they said that they had never seen such a case. Where a girl was betrothed to the obi, a lover had to buy a slave to cleanse the town and pay one bag to each ọkpalẹbo to purchase his intercession, twenty bags to the obi, ten to the ike ani, a goat for ani uku, another for Adubwe, a goat to ikẹnga orhẹze, one bag to each of the onotu, five in all, and three bags to ọmu's company. Where the wife of an obi committed adultery, both parties were hanged and their bodies redeemed by their kin at the price of one bag. They were buried in the ajoifia if this is not done. A cock, an aka bead, and a red feather, have also to be paid to Iyase.

At Nsukwa, where the customs are widely different, it is the lover who brings the girl to the ọkpalidumu to confess, and they offer to the mwọ. The husband need not be present.

IDEBWE.—There can be no doubt that the idẹbwe custom (p. 60) has spread southwards from the Ishan country, for it appears to have reached Asaba comparatively recently, and even now it is unknown, according to statements made to me, in g ashi and Ala. Under normal circumstances the idẹbwe is kept because there is no son, but at Asaba, Onitsha Olona, Obuluku, and Ubulubu, the possession of a son does not prevent the father from making one of his daughters idẹbwe.

A man cannot make his daughter idẹbwe under ordinary circumstances without some form of declaration. At Isele Asaba he calls his idumu and offers a goat; after this she will inherit her father's house and all his property to the exclusion of his brother; she may even take a title, though she may not become ọkpalẹbo. The same disability is imposed here, as elsewhere, on her son or sons.

At Onitsha Olona her father declares to the umunna that she is idẹbwe and builds a house for her; he reckons as her husband and will pay one bag to her ọkpala for her. If she has no male children she may make one of her daughters idẹbwe in her turn. If one wife has no male children she may pay the price of one of her daughters and keep her as idẹbwe; in this case, after the death of the father, one of the half brothers reckons as her husband.

At Idumuje Uboko, if a man dies without sons, his brother may offer a goat and in the presence of all the ẹbo declare one of the daughters to be idẹbwe. The mother of the idẹbwe has her children in ọma precisely as is the case with the children of a woman married in the ordinary way.

At Onitsha Ubwo a man can make one or more daughters idẹbwe, but if anyone has begun to pay bride price, this must be refunded and also the ifẹnru. If the idẹbwe bears only daughters the father's brother is the heir, and failing the father's brother, the head of the umunna. Where there are only daughters the father's brother arranges their marriage and takes the price.

At Ukunzu the father announces that his daughter is idẹbwe and at dawn he hands her over to the itokwẹlẹgwe (workers), and she joins them when they come out for work, bringing kola and tobacco for them.

At Obọmpa the father explains to the ẹbo and offers kola to the mwọ. He is placed in the position of husband to his daughter to such an extent that when he sacrifices to his ancestors be hands yams to his daughter which she has to bring to him as if she were his son-in-law. When she reaches marriageable age the share of the bride price which would normally go to her mother is given to her and her father also gives her goats for if'arụ, if'ọna, and other ordinary payments. If, after making one of his daughters idẹbwe, the father marries later and has a son, the child of the idẹbwe, even though he is the elder, comes second in the family. He would take his mother's property and would only get one cow from his father's property. If the idẹbwe bears no sons all her daughters must be given to husbands and the bride price goes to the heir of her father.

At Ubulubu a goat is sacrificed before the idumu when the girl reaches a marriageable age, but apparently it is known before this that the girl is to be made idẹbwe, for a man offers himself as a friend before the sacrifice is performed, brings ifẹnru, and works in her father's farm. At the "igwe" ceremony five yams go to the mother and five to the girl. On the following day the mother cooks and sends to the man and gives eight ngugu to buy meat for soup. The boy then calls his idumu to eat. Five ngugu are put in the soup pot, but this appears to be an irregular practice of which the elders do not approve. At puberty the go-between goes to ask for the girl, and just like an ordinary wife she gets a portion of the friend's farm for if'ubwo; the friend continues to give assistance to her father in the farm.

If a woman bears no sons she may make one of her daughters idẹbwe, and her eldest son, if she bears one, is entitled to a share of his grandfather's property. At the burial of his grandfather he acts in the same way as a son. If an idẹbwe has no son she can take her mother's property and make one of her daughters idẹbwe. The eldest son and daughter serve their mother's brother by the same father, the other sons and daughters serve their eldest brother.

At Ezi, as at Ukunzu, the idẹbwe joins the workers. The son of the idẹbwe can here become ọkpalẹbo.

If late in life the father gets a son by another wife, half of the father's property must go to him. If the father of a childless idẹbwe dies his brother and the childless idẹbwe share the property and bury him.

In some cases the father takes an oath to give the idẹbwe in marriage to her mbwa (friend), if she wishes, after she has borne children. The idẹbwe who bears only daughters can leave one as idẹbwe, but the others must be given to husbánds. The idẹbwe gets from her father the gifts which the husband ordinarily gives ; one bag is paid to whoever has her mother in ọma (p. 51) ; it is believed that if this were not handed over she would bear no children.

It is everywhere the rule that the idẹbwe is restricted to a single lover, and in many cases the lover is sworn not to run away with her nor take her to wife, nor to kill the woman, nor to steal from her father.

At Obọmpa the friend brings seven ọko to the father, who refuses them ; the same night he brings a calabash of palm wine and the girl is handed over to him ; it is a rule that neither father nor mother can receive money.

At Ezi in addition to other items of the oath the friend is sworn to declare to her father if she commits adultery. At Nsukwa, on the other hand, no oath of any sort is taken. Under ordinary circumstances, however, if a friend proves unsatisfactory, or if, for example, he quits the town, it is permissible for a girl to take some one else, but capricious changes are disapproved of just as much as what may be termed adultery, that is to say, irregular connections with others than the friend bound by oath.

At Ukunzu it appears to be the rule that the idẹbwe must remain with the mbwa for life. If she runs to another ẹbo the umunna of her mbwa may fight with the people of her new friend and take iyi (pp. 93, 100) there precisely as if she were a runaway wife.

At Idumuje Uboko the idẹbwe who goes to other men would be rebuked by her umunna, and if she persists the umunna may offer a goat to nze and make her marry the original friend. Here as elsewhere the woman selects the friend, who has, however, to be approved by her father or the umunna.

At Idumuje, which is close to the Ishan border, the customs differ in other respects also, for the friend takes no oath, and the mother, not the father, is in the place of the husband. In other cases marriage is permitted when the idẹbwe has borne two or three children. In this case she

G

leaves the children with her mother. The ordinary bride price is paid even when the friend marries her and the ifᶒnru go on as long as the wife lives.

At Onitsha Ubwo a calabash of oil, twenty yams and ten ngugu are given to the mother by the friend but nothing to the father. When enough children have been born the idᶒbwe is told to marry her mbwa, and the father may take one or two sons and give the rest to the mbwa. Properly speaking the decision rests with the idᶒbwe's father, but since the white man came the idᶒbwe herself has been claiming a voice in the matter. I was also told that the native court is giving all the children to the mbwa where he pays bride price, even though it has been agreed that he is to share the children with the father.

At Idumuje Ụnọ the mbwa may pay ten bags to the father, three bags to the mother and two bags to other relatives and marry the idᶒbwe if children have been born. As elsewhere, a goat has to be offered to the mwọ to reverse the position set up by the original sacrifice when the girl was made idᶒbwe.

At Ukunzu, when the girl has four children and wishes to marry her friend, a goat is sacrificed to nnadi (=umunadi), a hen is killed upon the long broom used by the workers and ten yams are also offered. The friend pays the ordinary price.

At Obọmpa the idᶒbwe may be offered as a wife to the friend, but if the male children of the father die after she has been married, the father cannot claim any children born in wedlock.

At Ubulubu after the idᶒbwe has borne three children, she may be given to a husband, but not necessarily to the friend. In some cases the father's heir gives her to a husband and takes bride price, but before this can be done she must have a son or daughter.

At Nsukwa the rule is once idᶒbwe always idᶒbwe. If she has no son she inherits nevertheless.

In many cases, notably at Isele Asaba, Onitsha Olona

Idumuje Ụnọ, Ubulubu and Nsukwa the idẹbwe is permitted to marry a wife precisely like an ordinary childless wife and thus raise up heirs to herself if she has no children of her own.

"WOMAN MARRIAGE."—This custom of woman marrying woman has practically the same distribution as the idẹbwe custom, that is to say, it does not appear to be found at Ala and g ashi. In the case of "ṅwunye okporo" (woman wife) an oath is required from the friend and adultery is forbidden, precisely in the same way as in the case of the idẹbwe, and in both cases when the girl is assigned to her friend the period of licence, which is normal in ordinary marriage customs, is unknown. There is a considerable amount of variation in the position of "ṅwunye okporo" in the different towns.

At Isole Asaba the "ṅwunye di" (woman husband) (H) consults her own people and they give her another girl (W) to give her husband, who pays for her ; if no near relative is available the woman pays for a girl. If a son is born he takes all the property of the husband, but under no circumstances may W go to the husband of H. If H's husband dies, W goes to his sons unless she is too young. If, however, instead of marrying within the umunna, H marries the eldest son of the dead man, W remains with her friend.

At Oboluku W must not come from the same ẹbo as H ; when H dies the husband cannot marry W, and if she has borne male children she would not marry again but would remain with her mbwa, and all children would belong to the dead woman, i.e., her husband. If she has borne no male children she is free to marry. If the husband of H dies, his heir takes charge of W, and she remains with her mbwa. The reason given for a woman marrying a woman was that she wished to have an heir, otherwise all her property would go to her people.

At Idumuje Uboko both the girl and her friend are sworn not to kill each other, and the friend undertakes not to run away with her or marry her, and he and the umunna to which H and her husband belong undertake jointly no to injure each other. When H dies she goes as a wife to the man who buries H, the friend being sent away. All H's property goes to her husband. At his death it all passes to the children of W. If, however, the children are adult at H's death they receive the property at once if they are sons. A somewhat interesting case was brought to my notice in which the female orhẹne of Nemonica, who was childless, engaged a wife, who was seized on the road when she was taking food to her H when she was sick in bed; this was about seven years ago. Since then she has borne two children, a boy and a girl, to the man who seized her, whose rights are not admitted by the girl's father. He says that the husband has not paid bride price and yet buried the dead; hence, as his daughter was not brought to H to bury, " the child is still alive for her."

At Idumuje Ụnọ I was told that the husband of H could hand W to one of his sons at the death of H. If only daughters were born to W, one of them might be made idẹbwe. At Onitsha Ubwo W goes to the husband when H dies.

At Ukunzu a childless woman takes wood as a suitor to the mother of a baby girl, and then tells her husband, who performs the rest of the service for her; but when the girl reaches marriageable age she is assigned to a friend with her consent and thereafter cannot change. He brings seven ọko for her and H gets from her husband a goat, cloth and three ngugu " to lead her to her mbwa." W lives in her own house in the compound of the husband and at birth H goes to name the child. If it is a male child he buries H; if it is a daughter she buries her in the same way and becomes idẹbwe. W must not be from the same ẹbo as H but may belong to the husband's ẹbo. If H dies W remains with her mbwa if she is of the same ẹbo as the husband of H, other- wise she may marry in his umunna. In a specific case which came under my notice, however, I was informed that she might marry the husband or one of his sons. If before the death of H no male child is born, H's property may go to a posthumous child. Till a child has been born W may not marry. If the child is a girl she becomes idǫbwe.

At O ǫ pa a son of W cannot become ǫkpalumunna nor be the first heir of H's husband if he has another son. If H dies W can go to the husband or be given to the son if she has borne no male children, otherwise she will remain with her friend, bearing children for the son. Here W must not belong to the ǫbo of the husband or of H.

At Ubulubu H serves like an ordinary suitor save that the husband undertakes the farm work. If the friend quarrels with W she is permitted to change, for they say "one person never finishes one head of nuts." When H dies W goes to the husband, or if she misbehaves in H's lifetime the same can be done, and H has then no more authority over her. W cannot come from the same ǫbo as H or her husband but can get a friend from another idumu of the same ǫbo. The children of W can take a share of the property of H's husband, such as a cow or seed yams or even a widow.

At Ezi W may be of the husband's ǫbo, for here the idumu is the exogamous unit. If W bears only daughters H can leave them only part of her property and part goes to her husband. If W is of the same idumu as the husband, when H dies, even if she has borne no children, she is given to a husband, who pays price for her.

At Nsukwa W can be taken from any ǫbo. If H dies she remains with her friend. She cannot marry.

V.—CRIMINAL LAW.

MURDER.—The ordinary rule in cases of murder was that the culprit had to hang himself, but it was also possible to pay compensation and hand over a woman to the brother of the murdered man, to be his wife and to raise up children in the place of the dead man.

At Asaba the culprit hanged himself, and his umunna buried him, but they did not lament for him. If the murderer and his victim were of the same quarter, the mother's people, Ikunne, of the dead man came to demand the murderer, who had to suffer death; no blood money could be taken. If the murderer ran, it was a signal for spoliation; trees were cut down and houses burned, though how far this right of retaliation extended I could not quite ascertain. If the murderer ran to another town they would fight with the town to which he went or put an alose down, Ogugu or Atakbe, to kill the people of the town.

In addition to murder, justifiable homicide and accidental homicide were recognised. If a thief came in the night he might be killed if he were caught in the act, but he would more often be wounded so that it would be easy to discover his identity. If a thief were killed under such circumstances it might be treated as murder in the absence of a witness. If one man attacked another on the road with intention to rob him, a wound might be given as a sign; if a thief were killed, the stolen property had to be put on his chest. If a man assaulted a pregnant woman and caused a miscarriage, he could be required to pay money or give a woman to the family as a wife, but it was not regarded as murder. A husband who killed his wife was guilty of murder, but not, according to one statement made to me, a woman who killed her husband.

If two men were on bad terms and A threatened B, A

might get into difficulties if evil befell B or his house, but would not, however, be hanged in the ordinary way; though if B met his death when out hunting with A, matters might be serious for the latter. A hunter who shot a man by accident was required to confess. He might offer money to the umunna of the dead man and they were free to accept or not, or a woman might be given as a wife.

If one ẹbo fought with another and a slave were killed, it was a case for compensation, monetary or in kind. If a slave killed a slave he might be hanged or taken to replace the dead man. If a slave killed a free man the owner might be hanged. It was, however, possible for a murderer to escape death if he could come to Odogu before knowledge of the murder was spread abroad. Odogu might then put an eagle's feather upon his head; this was equivalent to a declaration that the homicide was not a murder.

At Ọkpanam the ordinary rule with regard to murder was the same. If it was a case of homicide (Ọyọm) the man was not hanged if he confessed, provided there had been no previous palaver between the parties. He had to bury the dead man, give his daughter to wife, and make various other payments to the son of the man or his brother. For a " small man " who had taken no title of importance, the payment was two goats, one cock, one dog, one piece of cloth and powder; for ṅkpalo four goats, and one hen in addition to the other articles; for ẹze eight goats, two cocks, and two hens, all of which were used for the burial ceremonies. After taking this to the son of the dead man, the culprit gave drink to his ọbwọ and thanked his či that he had escaped death. If he killed a woman, he gave his daughter to the son or brother of the dead woman or to her husband, if she had a husband, and supplied materials for the burial rites as before. If the chosen girl objected and ran, her father explained to the man to whom she ran that she was being given in compensation for murder. She would then be given up and would have to remain with the husband to whom she was given. If one woman killed another accidentally, naturally a very rare occurrence, money only was paid in compensation. Her mother's people would take about £2 10s., and her father's people the same.

At Qkpanam there was a special functionary known as Ẹzobu. The head of a man killed in war was brought to him first, and if he refused to put chalk and feathers, it was a declaration that the killer was a murderer. If Isele people, for example, seized a girl as a wife and a man were killed in the struggle between the young men, the Ẹzobu might refuse the eagle's feather and permit the man to be hanged. The Isele people might come to his house and see him hanged, or might come after the event to identify the body before burial. It was incumbent upon a murderer to hang himself, for if anyone else hanged him it would be murder; if he ran, the Isele people came and were told that he had run. They could not claim another man in his place, but a girl would be paid over and eight or ten bags of cowries. This would be taken by the children of a u w a d a, and the brother of the dead man would receive a wife and his u m u n n a the money (to take qmu from their hands).

At Isele Asaba, if two ẹbo were fighting and one man killed another, the penalty was death; he would come to the open street and hang himself, though a rich man was permitted to hang himself in his own house. His own brother would plant two sticks and put a cross beam over them. Then Iyase and Odogu came and received 980 cowries. Odogu asked for the matchet with which the man had been killed and cut the corpse down with it. Then the brother took the corpse and lamented, saying, " You will never murder again, when you return to this world." If a murderer ran, his hosts had to look into the matter and hand him over, even if he were a relative. If he were not a relative, he would be handed over without enquiry, but in the latter case the sum of thirty bags would be paid for him, ten bags of which went to the host and twenty to the town. If the murderer were retained it would not necessarily mean war, but the farms would be spoilt and the trees cut down.

In a case of accidental homicide Odogu and Iyase enquired into the case, and if there had been no previous trouble, the town was called together and Iyase explained the circumstances. The culprit paid for the burial of the dead man. If there had been previous trouble, the umunna of the dead man brought iyi, and told the hunter to come and swear. If he took an oath, the matter was settled, but if he and his people were killed by the iyi, his people would come and beg, and his idumu would have to give a wife, or, if a sufficient sum of money were offered, the giving of a wife might fall through.

At Onitsha Olona, if a thief came to the farm or the house, they could shoot at night; in the day-time the proper course was to pursue him and call for help, but if they failed to do so, in the farm it was permissible to fire. The stolen object was put on his chest and the umunna of the dead man came and took his body. No payment was made on either side.

The Iyase had important functions in the case of murder. He would order the murderer to be brought, and if he were not brought he would seize the property of the idumu. All the onotu accompanied him and got a portion of the seized property. If a man killed one of his own umunna the onotu seized property, and the brother of the murderer helped the offender to give kola to the ǫkpalębo. One bag of cowries was paid to the head chief, one bag to Onirhe (p. 44), one bag to the okwęlęgwe. A woman was given to the brother of the dead man, she would be either the murderer's own daughter or his brother's. One bag of cowries and one goat was offered to the ani; the murderer might be hanged if he ran. If both were members of the same idumu he might be hanged, or the people of the murdered man might accept compensation. The hosts of a runaway murderer received five bags or more and when the murderer was seized there was no question of compensation. If both belonged to the same ębo, the murderer would be hanged unless he were an important man.

If the ǫkpalębo and the ikei ani considered that the interest of the ębo required that the murderer should not be killed, they would inform the town, and decide that compensation should be paid. If the murderer belonged to a different town, he was hanged if he was caught. If he escaped, the o n o t u sent a message and asked for him to be handed over; the proper persons to approach in the matter were the o n o t u in the other town. If they refused, the o n o t u of the murdered man's town seized a person, if possible, and then war came. Apparently in this case compensation was impossible. Peace between the two towns might be brought about when the farming time came.

In the case of accidental homicide during hunting, the Iyase seized the hunter's gun and outfit and the ordinary rule was followed.

At Ala the murderer was hanged even if the two parties belonged to the same i d u m u; his own u m u n n a brought him out, and the brother of the murdered man put the noose round his neck; if he ran, the houses of the ẹbo to which he belonged were burned and their trees wasted. His u m u n n a were sent after him to bring him back, and the ẹbo could not rebuild their houses until he was found; they had to remove to another spot if necessary. Farms could be made on the site of the old houses.

No compensation was payable, but the u m u n n a of the murderer might pay for respite. If necessary, the murderer's u m u n n a paid money to his hosts in order to gain possession of him. When two ẹbo fought and a man was killed, if the murderer was unknown, the town asked who began the trouble, and the man adjudged to be the culprit had to bring a woman for the brother of the dead man. If a woman caused palaver she might be handed over in person or her daughter in her place. If she had no daughter, her husband had to give a a daughter or obtain a girl by purchase.

In cases of accidental homicide, if the culprit confessed, compensation was paid, otherwise he was hanged. If a corpse was found, each ẹbo would enquire what hunters had gone out and each man would be called upon to state which road he had taken.

At Ibuzọ, if two ẹbo had a dance on the same day, they

occasionally met in the street. · If one or the other began to throw sand, a sign of contempt, a fight would be caused, and if a man were killed the murderer had to be seized by his own umunna and handed over to be hanged. His ẹbo collected to help his umunna to look for him; when he was found the men of his ẹbo beat drums and the murderer danced round the town and then hanged himself in his own house. His umunna cut him down and buried him after killing ewu ikẹṅga, saying, " It is a deaf child that killed himself, it is what he got from his či." The rule would be the same if a man killed another from the same umunna. If the murderer ran, his umunna gave money to his host to release him, or if not, they handed over a woman to the family of the dead man, and the brother of the murderer defrayed the expenses of the burial. The murderer could return to his home only after many years.

If a slave killed a free man the owner was hanged, or the slave could be handed over and killed at the burial. Then the owner would pay compensation, but before doing so, he would have to pay £2 10s. to the ọkpalẹbo.

The olinzẹle were summoned in the cases of suspected murder, and asked the culprit to drink inyi. He was taken to Onitsha by his accuser and the umunna of both parties accompanied them. If the man died he was buried in the bush at Onitsha. If not, he came home and rejoiced, and the accuser paid 5s. compensation to him. Where one hunter killed another, it was usually considered that he did it maliciously and capital punishment would be inflicted. They never fired at a thief, but tried to seize him or recognise him.

If a man cutting palm nuts dropped them on the head of a person below and killed him, no compensation would be payable, but the man responsible would bring a goat for the dead man's ikẹṅga. If a husband caused his wife to miscarry, there would be no palaver, but if another man were responsible, it would be regarded as murder ; even if the wife died the husband would not be regarded as responsible. He would be merely required to complete payment of the bride price if he had not already done so, and bury his wife in the ordinary way.

At g ashi, if one man killed another in a fight, the obi took the object which caused the fight, if there were one, and the murderer hanged himself. A goat and one ngugu four uku were paid to the obi to remove his seat (irhe ǫbwala, that is, take it back to his own house after going to the murderer's house) and the same to the Iyase. If the murderer ran, his own brother might be killed or one of his umunna; the murderer could then return and bury the man killed in his place; no payment could then be demanded. If the quarrel were caused by a woman, a horn would be blown and the town met. The Iyase ordered people to cook for the murderer, and he hanged himself. His people cut him down and buried him, and the woman who was responsible for the trouble was given to the obi as his wife. A sister of a man could not be taken as compensation, nor her child nor a person of the same idumu. The family could pay money to the obi to settle the case before he called the assembly ; one woman, or two cows or a slave was the normal amount.

After the people had assembled, the murderer's brother would have to pay two women, and if either of them ran, the matter was reopened. If both parties were of the same ǫbo, two cows were paid or two daughters handed over. If one first cousin killed another, the culprit could not be hanged; such cases happened occasionally in games. A husband could not be hanged for killing a wife, but if he had not completed payment of the bride price, the necessary sum had to be handed over together with an additional amount, equal in value to one cow. But this was only due if the bride price had not been completed.

If a woman killed a man, she might suffer the penalty herself, or her brother could die in her stead. Two women, wives of the same husband, sometimes killed each other. In one case that was brought under my notice, the woman was not hanged, on the ground that both women were the property of their husband. The murderess took her daughter and gave her as a wife to the son of the woman whom she had killed. He must, therefore, presumably have been a step-son of the husband. The husband agreed to give up the money, but afterwards married another wife.

At Oboluku Iyase seized a murderer and saw that he hanged himself, If he used a matchet to commit the murder it was seized and sent to the obi. The people of the dead man notified the obi and seized the murderer; he was then asked to justify his action, and if it was found to be wilful murder, he was asked to hang himself, if not, he handed over a woman and paid money to the ikei ani. If the two parties were of the same umunna, the murderer's house and those of his brothers were burned if he ran. If they were not of the same umunna, the houses and property of his umunna would be spoiled, or if the idumu joined with the umunna, the whole idumu was drawn into the conflict.

If the murderer could not be found, the umunna took iyi to the street in which he lived. Chalk was taken from the alose and thrown on the ground after being powdered. Stones were taken from the iyi, and the houses of the murderer and his brothers rubbed with chalk. In order to settle the matter, a wife was given to the brother of the dead man and they were asked to take the alose away. The doctor said what animal should be killed, and peace was finally made when the woman had borne a child. In the ease of accidental homicide a woman was handed over.

At Idumuje Uboko the onotu went to seize the property of a murderer and broke down his house. If he ran, the property of the umunna was also seized and their houses broken down; they might even be made prisoners till the murderer was brought, and, if necessary, they had to pay a sum of money to recover him. He was handed over to the onotu, who brought him to his house and fixed a rope for him, or a hole might be made in the wall and a rope passed through it, which the onotu pulled till the man died, If the murderer could not be recovered, a daughter or some other woman had to be handed over and money paid to the onotu. If after this a man returned, he gave a goat, to be sacrificed to the ani uku. If a woman were handed over, the houses were not broken down, and it was possible to hand over a daughter of the murderer temporarily, in order to gain a respite until he was found. If both parties were of the same ẹbo, so that the daughter could not marry the brother of the murdered man, she might, nevertheless, be accepted and handed to a friend.

If two men fought over a woman and one were killed, the woman was sent to the obi as a wife, or, if she were of his own quarter, was handed to Iyase or Odogu, or, failing that, the obi might take money from her father and give the woman back to him. She would not be given to her husband, but remained in her father's house or ran to another idumu. The husband would have to pay compensation in addition to losing his wife. A husband who killed his wife was a murderer, and might be hanged, or required to give a daughter to the father of his wife, for her father gave his daughter as a wife, and not in order that she might be killed.

In cases of accidental homicide, a goat and cloth were given to the brother of the dead man, and a goat offered to the ani· uku by the ikei. If the man were not killed on the spot, the culprit had also to bring whatever the doctor ordered to offer to the mwọ. When a murderer had to be hanged, Iyase and Odogu brought him out.

At Idumuje Ụnọ the onotu had to fetch the murderer, and, if the latter ran, his umunna had to watch for him. Their houses might in the meantime be broken down and burned. If he were not found, the umunna begged the ikei ani to help, and gave a daughter to the family of the murdered man. The murderer could then return. If a hunter killed a man by mistake, the onotu were informed, and heard the case with the ikei ani. The culprit handed a he-goat and cloth to the brother of the murdered man for the burial ceremonies and gave a daughter.

At Onitsha Ubwo, the quarter of the murdered man went and burnt the houses of the umunna. The Iyase took him to the place where he was born, and he was hanged from a tree. If, however, 5s. were paid to the olinzẹle, they might allow him to pay compensation. If a hunter killed another man accidentally, he lamented all the way home. He paid one dog, one cock, and two pieces of cloth to the family of the dead man, and offered food to the corpse; no other compensation was due. If a husband killed his wife he was hanged.

At Ukunzu a murderer would often commit suicide without further trouble. The umunna of the dead man went to see the corpse of the murderer and then buried their dead. If he did not at once commit suicide, the onotu were notified, and the culprit usually hanged himself before they came. If not, they seized him, broke his house down and seized his property. The onotu would bind him or allow him to hang himself, and then, if he were bound, his umunna would loose him, and tell him to hang himself. If he ran the ẹbo pursued him, broke down his house and seized his property, but this only on the day of the murder. If after three years he had not been found, his umunna paid compensation—three bags to obi, three to onotu, and one bag to ọmu; then a daughter could be handed over to the umunna of the dead man, and the obi sacrificed a goat before the ani uku; both umunna swore to keep the peace. The goat was shared between the obi and the ogẹnani (Onirhe) of the onotu, each getting one share; then the murderer could return. Justifiable homicide was recognised. When a thief was recognised, it was permissible to fire poisoned cross-how bolts. The poison was made at Obodo and Onitsha Ubwo.

At O ọ pa, if a murderer ran, the umunna of the dead man broke down the houses of the murderer's umunna and informed the enotu; when the murderer was taken, he tied a rope to his house and hanged himself; as at Onitsha Ubwo, a man who had killed a leopard was summoned to cut him down. One cock and seven ǫko were paid to the ǫmalegwe; if the murderer was not found, no compensation was payable. If the man were killed in a fight, ten bags were paid to the onotu and obi and a woman handed over. If the two parties were of the same umunna, the murderer paid money to the onotu and handed over a woman, who was kept as idębwe. The murderer might, however, say that he preferred to hang, as he could not live at peace with his neighbours.

The Iyase decided what should be done if a man of the town killed a stranger. If they decided that it was a case of murder, the Iyase sent to the ębo to seize the man and take him to the boundary, where he was hanged in the presence of the onotu of the injured town, and the umunna of the murderer paid one bag. If he were not hanged, ten bags and a woman were paid to the ębo.

In the case of accidental homicide the onotu and obi had to hear evidence. The dead man's dying declaration would be decisive. The brother of the dead man had the chief voice in the decision. In the case of accident the hunter was required to bring in the dead man's gun, lamenting all the way. He paid ten bags to the onotu and the ikei ani, handed over a woman, and gave a mat, cloth, and string of cowries for the burial ceremonies.

At Ubulubu I was told that no case of murder had been known since the town was founded.

At Ezi the Iyase decided whether compensation should be paid or the murderer be hanged. The murderer was seized by his umunna and handed over to be hanged in " obi's street " from an nkata tree ; the head of the onotu put the rope on his neck for him. The onotu received a cock, an aka bead, an eagle's feather, and seven ǫko to cut the body down. The runaway was caught by his own umunna or purchased for the sum of 7s. 6d. or 10s. from his host. The umunna seized property from the relatives of the murderer, and continued doing so at intervals for 12 months, if he were not caught, sending money also to the onotu and the ikei ani to beg. If a woman was handed over and one bag of cowries, the two umunna met in the street and the loser swore not to seize any more property; the murderer could then return. If the murderer hanged himself, compensation of some sort had to be paid. If the murderer were sick, his umunna hastened to bring him to be hanged. The umwada of the dead man threw iyi down in the precincts of the murderer's house and those of his umunna and removed them when the case was settled. To do this chalk was taken and cowries tied round it, and they said to the iyi: " Come, we take you to Ukbo that you may do no more harm." Then the foreheads of the umunna were touched with chalk, with the words: " We take back the curse," and chalk was put upon the iyi. If both parties were of the same ẹbo the onotu seized property, and the murderer was hanged as before. If he ran and a woman was handed over, a goat might be offered to the ani and the murderer might return. If both belonged to the same umunna a man might still be hanged, but if a woman was handed over she was kept as idẹbwe.

In cases of accidental homicide compensation was paid and a goat sacrificed to the ani. The culprit had to cry out and call for witnesses; if he did not do so he hanged himself in his house. Killing a cow was reckoned as murder; one bag was paid to each of the onotu and two cows to the owner, and a goat and one bag was taken to the ani.

At Nsukwa a murderer hanged himself without more ado. If he ran nothing was done to the family, but notice was given to the town he ran to, that they must hand him over. Compensation of a woman and some £5 was payable, and they thought that this might be paid even where a husband murdered his wife. Accidental homicide was settled by payment of compensation.

THEFT.—Generally speaking there were two ways of dealing with theft in the Asaba district. In the first place the loser together with his umunna would take steps to recover the property, or secondly he might call upon the Nzẹle or other dignitaries of the town to interfere.

At Asaba, anyone who saw a thief in the act was at liberty to fire at him, but only with the intent to wound. If the thief had no weapons he would ask for mercy, whereupon the witnesses would go and report to the head of the thief's quarter. The thief was compelled to give a goat, known as Ewu ikẹṅga, and sacrifice to the ikẹṅga of the loser. Then the loser was at liberty to seize the property of anyone in the quarter of the thief, and only stopped seizing if the quarter promised reparation. Under ordinary circumstances the thief would hand over his daughter as a wife to the loser; in the case of a kinsman the stolen object would simply be handed back or its value. If the thief ran the umunna of the loser would seize all the property of the thief's umunna, unless the latter begged the former to wait till they could catch the thief. For a second offence the ọkpalẹbo of the thief would report him to the town and he would be fined, one share going to the town and another to the company to which he belonged, and if he had no effects he might be sold. For the third offence he might be hanged or drowned in the river with a stone on his chest. It was the duty of the ọmu or market queen to be present at the sale or drowning.

At Ọkpanam, if a thief came in the night it was legal to fire at him with the intent to wound him, or a quarter-staff might be used to break his leg. If a watcher in a farm saw anyone moving about in a suspicious way he could fire at him and kill him. In that case a yam would be laid upon his chest and the thief's umunna would come and see the corpse and take him away for burial. If the theft were committed in the daytime the thief would be caught and brought home; the loser would go to the idumu of the thief and seize a goat for sacrifice to his ikẹṅga; he could then take at will any property either of the thief or of his umunna.

A thief who came from another ẹbo might be seized and sold; in fact his own ẹbo would tie him up and take him to the ẹbo of the loser. A kinsman, however, could not be sold as a slave, but the loser and his umunna would keep on seizing property till the thief handed over a daughter as a wife. This was known as ibuči orhi. An habitual thief would be expelled from his idumu and become a wanderer. Under ordinary circumstances a theft in the market was a minor offence, but at Qkpanam it appeared that they could seize property when a man stole in the market. In the case of a woman they would take one bag of cowries to settle the matter.

Ordinarily in the case of a woman thief no heavy penalty was inflicted; her husband would beg the people. If, however, she became an habitual thief her husband would send her home to her father. If a small girl took to stealing, a very exceptional circumstance apparently, she would never find a husband; the umunna of any suitor would warn him against marrying her. Apparently a widow was never killed or sold, only expelled from the community; but I was told that everyone would rejoice when she died.

When a thief denied his guilt the sass wood ordeal might be tried. They sent to Ala for dibi'inyi (a doctor of sass wood), and all the town gathered at the beginning of the farm road or at an artificial hillock made when grass is cleared. The inyi was pounded in a mortar by a doctor's assistant, and the doctor put chalk and explained the charge against the accused. Water was then added, and the liquid was then strained in a small basket, known as irhadi, into a calabash from which the doctor gave the accused man to drink. If any remained over they would loose the plaited hair on the crown of his head (ososu) and pour the inyi over it. Then all went away and the man's idumu took him home; if he died on the road they threw his body into the ajoifia and burned him; if, however, he survived seven days, he called his company and gave them palm wine, at the same time offering thanks to his či. If the accused man died the loser would seize his property and that of the umunna, and the brother or children of the thief would give a woman to the loser as his wife.

Where a theft was committed and the thief was unknown, enquiry would be made among the neighbours if there was a witness who could throw light upon the matter, and after this the ẹbo was called three successive times to a meeting. The loser got iyi alose, different alose that is, for the purpose of cursing the thief. He then asked the alose to find and kill the thief. If after this a man fell sick, a doctor divined to find out the cause of his illness. The sick man's people would beg and the loser would demand as much compensation as he pleased. The thief could not return the stolen object, but had to pay for it.

At Isele Asaba, if a thief belonged to another ẹbo the loser could not seize the person, but could take the property of the thief or of anyone of the same umunna. He could also seize cows, slaves, and other property, or put iyi in his farm and inform the thief of what he had done. This would mean that the thief would not venture to use his farm. Or he might go to the ẹze or Iyase and put the farm in their charge with the same result. None of the stolen property would be handed back, but the thief would give his daughter to the loser to wife. A thief in the same ẹbo was fined ten bags of cowries, and in the same idumu three bags. Even in the same umunna a fine was imposed and a meeting called to warn the offender. An habitual thief was sold. A thief could be killed either by day or by night in the farm and the yam laid upon his chest. If a thief came in the night to a house they could not fire, but the following day would send word to his ẹbo, who would send a good goat back known as ewose or ewu ikẹnga. After sacrificing this the loser would begin to fire guns, and then send to the thief who was compelled to pay for the powder.

In the case of a woman the fine was fixed at ten bags only, because a woman thief only brought trouble on her husband, and the same rule prevailed in the case of a child. It was, however, stated that girls seldom stole. In the case of a woman stealing in the market, the case was settled by the ọmu. They never heard of a man stealing in the market; men did not go to the market; if men began to frequent the market, the Iyase would close it till the men gave up going.

Another way of dealing with a thief was for the loser to complain to the Anikamado. Iyase and Ago, the head chief, chose twenty men from each ẹbo, who had to be of unblemished reputation. The ẹze (head) anikamado commanded them, and their duty was to act as a watch committee for the town. If the loser found the thief he would pay the ẹgo onyama, that is, the informant's money, which had to be refunded by the thief. If this was not done the anikamado were informed, and they caused a flute to be sounded and sent for the thief. He would send men of his idumu to represent him, fearing to go himself lest he should be killed or sold. The anikamado inflicted a fine of twenty bags, and the thief also paid the value of the article and the ẹgo onyama. This was for a first offence.

For a second offence the anikamado would go and sack the house of the thief, who had to send money to settle the case before he could return to the town. For a third offence the anikamado would seize the thief and either sell or kill him. The fines were divided by the Ikei ani, and a portion also went to the loser. After reporting to the anikamado, a man could not seize the property of the thief, but he might seize things if the thief sent people to beg him not to inform the anikamado.

At Onitsha Olona a thief had to pay a fine, fixed by the loser, in default of which he might be sold if the town so decided. In the case of a kinsman, apparently, nothing was done. A woman who stole might be sold unless her husband paid her fine; a young boy who stole was flogged or starved. The fine for stealing corn was less than the fine for stealing a cow or a goat. If the town did not hear of the offence three bags settled the case, or five bags if the town heard of it. For a second offence the fine was ten bags, and for a third offence the thief was hanged or sold.

An alternative procedure in the case of a theft was to inform the o n o t u, whereupon Iyase would fix the fine, and the o n o t u and the i k e i a n i divided the money. If a thief came from another town he would be seized and held till his people redeemed him at a price fixed according to the stolen object. If he were not redeemed he would be sold as a slave. If a thief escaped his people had to bring him or the loser might seize a person and sell him if he were not redeemed.

At Ala it was forbidden to shoot at a thief in the house· If he were not seized and held, his u m u n n a were informed in the morning and the fine was £10 or in default a woman had to be handed over as a wife. They could, however, fire at a thief in the farm and put the stolen yams on his chest. Apparently, both in the farm and elsewhere, it was necessary to wait until the thief had actually laid his hands upon the object that he proposed to steal. The people of the thief would bury him and his death wiped out the offence; no payment would be made and if the thief were not of the same i d u m u he might be sold in default of paying the fine. In this case the u m u n n a of the thief could sell a man from the u m u n n a of the loser, if he subsequently committed a theft; the loser would not, as a rule, complain to the Iyase or o n o t u. It would usually happen that if the thief were an undesirable his u m u n n a would not intervene to protect him. In minor cases such as the theft of corn, kola, bananas and even fowls no fine was inflicted but the thief was abused. People would shout every morning and evening for a month : U U U, until he was ashamed to go out. If the thief ran, the loser would call upon the umunna to find him ; if they failed to do so they would seize one of the u m u n n a and sell him ; a boy under the age of 20 would be flogged. In the case of a woman who stole yam sticks for firewood, the Okute took charge of the farm and closed it to the woman.

At Ibuzọ the loser seized a goat in the ẹ bo of the thief. After that he seized property of the thief until the latter sent to beg and paid compensation of about twenty bags, together with ẹgo o n y a m a and other costs; in default of compensation the thief might be hanged in ẹ k e market. A theft of corn was on a somewhat different footing and was punished by a fine of £2 10s.; but otherwise all thefts were regarded as equal in the sight of the law. A thief, they said, must have been lazy and slept instead of working. They never sold thieves as slaves; a thief in the market got off lightly for they only shouted at him and abused him.

At g ashi it was permissible to shoot a thief in the night. In the daytime the thief would be recognised and information given to his umunna if he were not seized; the next day ¡the ewu ose or ewu ikęṅga (P. 98) would be killed with a matchet in the ębo of the thief. The meat was boiled and mixed with salt, oil and ground pepper, and offered to the ikęṅga; after the sacrifice of the goat a slave belonging to the thief, or his wife, or even his brother's wife might be seized or any other property at will, such as cows, goats, etc., or even an ornament from his wife's neck. This went on until a woman was brought as wife, or money in her place, which could be utilised as payment of bride price. Then the parties took an oath, the one not to go on seizing and the other not to take the wife away. If this were not done a person could be seized and sold. Habitual thieves were sold and all thefts were regarded as equal. Anyone who stole in the market was abused but suffered no further penalty. A known thief would probably be unable to get a wife. for the girl's father would regard it as throwing his daughter away.

It was comparatively seldom that women were guilty of theft; if one wife took the property of another wife of the same husband he could rebuke her but not refuse food or inflict any other penalty upon her, for it was not regarded as theft.

At Oboluku a thief might be shot at in the night if he did not answer the challenge, and the stolen object would be put on his chest. The stealer of a cow was regarded in the light of a murderer, and if he were shot, the gun used was handed to the Iyase as a deodand. If the thief were not shot the loser and his umunna might go to the thief's house and accuse him. When the thief was tired of having things seized he would offer money to the Ikei to help him to settle the case.

A fine of four goats would be paid to the loser but he might refuse them and seize a person. This would cause a conflict between the two ẹbo and the thief would have to pay the cost of the stolen article and an additional fine of five bags.

An alternative procedure was to report the case to the Iyase, who seized and kept the thief. If he wished to redeem himself he paid a fine of twenty bags and three bags for akabwọ, that is, the seat of the i·kei ani. The loser might seize property before reporting to the Iyase, and if he had a grudge against the thief, might go on seizing without reporting the matter all. If the matter were not reported, Iyase, if he heard of it, reported the matter to obi, who instructed him to keep an eye upon the proceedings. If the thief refused to go to Iyase, Ozọma and Iyase went to his house and seized him. A thief who was unable to pay his fine would sometimes pawn himself to raise the money, failing that he might be hanged ; in the time of the present Iyase three men suffered this penalty ; an habitual thief would certainly be hanged. In addition to inflicting the punishment of death, the Iyase and ikei ani might also seize property and persons, more especially where the thief deliberately refused to restore the stolen property or pay for it.

At Idumuje Uboko a thief might be shot in the night and the loser would then shout to alarm his neighbours ; the umunna of the thief took his corpse and buried him. If the loser seized the thief, the thief paid the value of the stolen object together with a fine of seven to ten bags reward to the informer. For a theft of corn five bags were paid to the informer and three bags to the ikei. If the loser were not satisfied he might refuse to accept the fine fixed by the ikei and the ikei might then say to him : " Plant your own seed, you or your children will reap it." If the thief refused to pay, the loser might seize a person and put a lose in the street of the thief's umunna or seize a goat.

An habitual thief brought trouble on his umunna and his ẹbo, for their goats and their property would be seized by the loser and his umunna after the ikei had fixed the amount of the fine and the thief did not pay it. The umunna of the thief would meet and bring the matter to the notice of the ikei ani. The thief would then be called and tied up and sold to another town, half the money going to the loser and half to the ikei ani; the price might be twenty or twenty-five bags, or for a young man forty bags; a girl about marriageable age might be worth even more.

At Idumuje Ụnọ a thief who denied his guilt was taken to the obi, who called upon him to swear; if he refused to do so he was found guilty. The reward to the informer was ten bags and the thief also paid twice the value of the stolen object. If a goat were stolen seven goats would be handed to the loser in addition to the stolen one. In the case of a theft by a person or persons unknown two ọfọ were taken to the place where the object has been stolen and curses were uttered against the thief in the presence of the ẹbo. Each person brought blacksmith's materials or an alose or mwọ. Then the ọfọ would be put across the farm road in order to kill the thief. Passers by would say: "Ọfọ lie in wait for the one they set you for."

At Onitsha Ubwo the loser received compensation, possibly 25s. if the theft was a serious one, and the town might decide to sell an habitual thief; if an informer were concerned in the matter the thief paid his fee as well. According to one statement the thief was never taken before the Olinzẹle, but I was also informed that the loser went to the obi of the town, who summoned the ikei ani to meet in his house. They settled the amount to be paid, which included 25s. to themselves.

In the case of a thief who denied his guilt, the inyi ordeal was tried. If the accused met his death in this way, his brothers paid the fine to the loser, but the town claimed nothing. If, on the other hand, the thief were declared innocent, the accuser paid ten bags compensation to him.

Other ordeals were known in Onitsha Ubwo. Medicine might be obtained and mixed with water in a vessel; a leaf was torn in half and put in the water, and if the two fragments floated and joined together the thief was adjudged guilty, if not, innocent. Another form of ordeal was probably derived from Benin City, where it is known by the same name, ịta. A fowl's feather was taken and smeared with medicine and a doctor tried to pass it through the tongue of an accused person; if it came out he was adjudged innocent; if it remained fixed after three times he was held guilty.

At Ukunzu shooting at a thief was forbidden, save with a cross-bow. If a thief were seized he was taken home and the ebo summoned. If he were of the same ẹbo as the loser, the ikei collected their mwọ before ani and the thief was called upon to swear never to steal again; he was fined three bags, half of which went to the loser and half to the ẹbo. If he were not of the same ẹbo the obi was informed, who summoned the onotu. The ikei had to meet before the ọgwa and a fine of five bags was inflicted upon the thief, together with five bags for the informer. If the fine were not paid a person might be seized, but he might not be sold; he was merely held as a pawn till the fine was paid; two bags out of five went to the owner, the rest to the town. Property was never seized in Ukunzu.

In the case of an unknown thief the usual method of cursing was adopted, and if it took effect he came to the loser and offered his daughter. He also gave kola and chalk to the loser, which were offered to the alose, and the sacrificer said: "A man has paid his debt, I change you so that you may take no effect."

If a man denied his guilt, inyi might be given or ịta tried; a third method of ordeal was known as Ifẹnza; a cow's tail was taken and stirred in medicine. A doctor then smeared the medicine on the eyes of the accused, or, more probably, flicked the face of the accused with the cow's tail, and called upon the alose to hold the thief. If, after this, a man could open his eyes he was adjudged innocent; if he were guilty and the suggestion took effect his eyes would remain closed.

At Obọmpa a loser seized the thief and fixed the compensation, which might be twenty bags, but if the obi and the ikei ani fixed the fine the thief had to be taken before them. Ten bags went to them and five to the owner, together with the value of the stolen object and the informer's fee. The informer, of course, had to bear witness if he were summoned by the obi and the ikei ani.

If a thief denied his guilt he might take an oath before the mwǫ or alose in the presence of the onotu and the ikei ani. He could, for example, swear before Okboku in the obi's house or the Ani uku. The accused had to bring a goat, which was offered by the obi after the supposed thief had made an offering of kola. The accused knelt before the ani and ate the heart raw; if nothing happened within three months he fired a gun and sacrificed to his či, and generally showed his satisfaction. The accuser had then to go to the informer and demand money to hand to the accused for ewo or hi, that is to wash the thief; this amounted to ten bags, and the informer's fee was also returnable. If, on the other hand, the accused man died the fines and rewards were payable exactly as if he had confessed.

A thief could be fired on at night, and if he were killed the stolen object put on his chest. In the farm it was permissible to fire at the thief if he were the stronger man. An alarm might be given at night and the idumu would turn out to search for the thief.

Several methods of ordeal were known. In the case of the ifęnza, if the accused were unable to open his eyes, more medicine was made and put on his eyes as before, with the words, "If you stole, let your eyes be opened," and then he could not fail to open his eyes.

At Ezi a thief aimed at hushing the matter up. He would offer money to the loser and return the stolen object; a fine, however, could not be taken from one of the same umunna. If, however, the matter became public, a meeting of the ębo was called and the thief compelled to pay the value of the stolen object, together with a fine fixed by the ębo, shared equally between the ębo and the loser. If a cow had been stolen, two cows were repaid, one bag to each onotu, and a goat was sacrificed to the ani. If corn were stolen a man of the same umunna would only be abused. A man might, however, go to the corn and cut some, provided he made a mark with his foot in the farm, to show where he had been, and subsequently informed the owner. If the ǫbo heard of a theft of corn a fine of 7s. 6d. might be imposed, one third of which went to the owner. In the case of a theft of yams or corn by a man of another ǫbo, the owner might demand ten bags and seize a person if the money were not paid, but could not, however, sell the person whom he had seized.

In the farm a cross-bow with a poisoned bolt might be used to fire at a thief. They had never seen guns used, they informed me, but there was not, necessarily, any objection to firing on a thief. A spiked trap might also be made in the farm path and covered with leaves and earth. A yam thief might be shot on the road and the basket of yams be put on his chest. If a thief came to the house at night he might also be shot; if a goat were the stolen object it might be tied to his leg or put on his chest; when his umunna came to take away his corpse, they would take the goat also. A member of the same umunna could not publicly accuse a thief unless it were habitual. Then the onotu would be informed. He could not, however, be sold even in this case; a fine would be inflicted, and, if necessary, the thief had to pawn himself in order to raise the money. A pawn who stole was in the position of a slave, and his master had to pay for him. If he died before he redeemed himself, two long brooms were tied to his hands and his brother buried him, apparently, however, only if the debt had previously been repaid.

An unknown thief is searched for in the following way: A loser strips himself and girds himself with dry banana leaves; he then puts a vessel on his head with alose in it and fire on the top. During my stay at Ezi I saw a man marching round the town in this guise but failed to persuade him to stand while I got my camera. If after the thief has thus been cursed a man falls sick a fine is arranged to settle the matter. If the accused dies before the fine is paid, his relatives bring his property and put it before the a l o s e. The loser is at liberty to select anything that takes his fancy. After all articles of any value have been taken a fine has to be paid in addition by the u m u n n a, and they beg that the curse may be taken off.

A thief who denied the informer's evidence might be put to the ordeal by sass wood, indirectly. A cock was taken and a decoction poured into its mouth; if it died the thief paid the fine and the informer's fee; if, on the other hand, he was declared innocent, he received e w o s e and compensation from ten bags upwards. Another method was to put kola on i y i; the accused took it in his own hand and ate calling on i y i to kill him, if he were guilty, in three months. If i y i did not hold him he offered to his či, but could not demand compensation from his accuser. If, on the other hand, he died, his u m u n n a would ask to have the curse taken off before they attempted to bury him, and offered money to have this done, If they buried the thief before doing so the curse would follow them. If the ordeal of ifǫnza were tried it was believed that a guilty person's eyes would not close; he blinked and they turned red like fire. This effect was blown from his eyes by the doctor if the culprit paid him three n g u g u, about 1s.

At Nsukwa a thief was tied up and paid a fine of £2 10s. or less; half would go to the i k e i a n i, together with the value of the stolen object.

LAWBREAKING: *Assault.*—At Qkpanam and generally where the ǫze title is known, an assault on an ǫze or even abuse was punished by a fine. Young men or even n k p a l o (p. 54) could fight, and women could also fight in the market, but if an ǫze were assaulted three goats were sacrificed, one for the culprit to the a n i u k u, one to the n z e (see p. 51) and one to the ndičie. One chicken was also required to cleanse the ǫze before the a n i.

At Onitsha Olona, if one man assaulted another with a

matchet, he paid the expenses if he inflicted a severe wound ; if the injury were a minor one the onotu fixed the penalty. Any assault on an ǫkpala, however, was punished by a fine of 25s. and one goat. Four bags were divided between the onotu and the other ǫkpala. An assault upon the head wife of an ǫkpala was punished by a fine of one bag, and one bag to the head wives of the ngwẹku (ǫkpala) of the ẹbo.

At Ibuzǫ there was no fine for an assault with a matchet except in the case of an ẹze, when the culprit had to pay three goats for the matchet, which was sacrificed by the ẹze to his mwǫ, one ram to clean up the blood and one cock that had crowed. If two obi fought all the obi came and they paid fines to each other. If a young man abused an elder the oke ẹbo called him and ordered him to buy a goat and send it to the man whom he had abused. There was no fine unless for-bidden things were said such as "ǫro nwunyeze;" an isimwǫ forbade the same things as an ẹze's wife.

Trespass.—There does not appear to be any definite law as to trespass; if a cow is found trespassing on a farm the owner of the farm is told he does not make his fence strong enough. In the same way the damage to persons by animals is not a subject for compensation. If a goat knocks a child down at Ala the mother can tie the goat up and if the child dies takes possession of the goat. If a goat eats yams the owner of the yams may cut a piece out of the goat's ear but he gets no compensation.

At Okpanam if a cow gores and kills a child the cow may be shot and the father receives the meat but the owner is not held responsible ; if the child is not killed the father can cut the cow with a matchet; if a goat hurts a child the mother may rub pepper in the goat's eyes; if a dog bites an ẹze it may be killed, but it may bite a child with impunity.

VI.—SLAVERY.

General.—There was as usual a difference between male and female slaves. Female slaves, as far as I could gather, never had a free day on which they could work for themselves, whereas male slaves usually had a free day or sometimes two, and could under certain circumstances be free of work altogether, though they still remained in the status of a slave. The marrying of a wife made a certain amount of difference to a male slave, inasmuch as his master usually accorded him more free time. In the case of a female slave marriage often meant that she was transferred to her husband's house and only gave ifǫnru to her master at certain periods. This of course was only the case where husband and wife belonged to different masters, that is to say, where the husband, or his master, did not purchase his slave wife.

Work Days.—Subject to the qualifications above mentioned, that a married slave, who had of course his own farm and was rearing up children for his master, the work days of a slave were as follows. (It must be remembered that one day of the week, which may vary according to the town or quarter, is reckoned as a rest day. The slave was free to work or not as he pleased. At Ibuzǫ, however, on the rest day ęke, farm work might not be done. The children and slaves met and went hunting, fishing, etc.):—

	Oye.	Afǫ.	Nkwǫ.	Ęke.
Asaba ...	+			
Okpanam ...	+	+	+	+
Isele Asaba ...	+	+	+	+
Onitsha Olona...	+	+		
Ala ...	+	+		
Ibuzǫ ...	+		+	

	Oye.	Afǫ.	Nkwǫ.	Ẹke.
Ogwashi ...	+	+	+	+
Oboluku ...	+	+	+	+
.Idumuje Uboko	+	+	+	
Idumuje Onǫ ...	+	+	+	+
Ukunzu ...	+	+	+	
Obǫmpa ...	+	+	+	+
Ezi	+	+		
Nsukwa ...	+		+	

Ubulubu had one free day.

Purchase.—At Isele Asaba, when a man wished to purchase a slave, he gave notice to his friends in case they had a slave that they wished to dispose of, and also sent to neighbouring towns. In some places, notably Ubulubu, when a slave was purchased, his master sacrificed to his ikẹṅga a ram, a cock and a goat. Other slave owners were called and also pawned persons and their masters; kola was offered to the ikẹṅga and the victims killed. The slave's head was shaved by the adẹbo and his hair put upon the ikẹṅga; after this the owner tied a string of cowries on his right hand. When a slave was purchased the seller had to keep his cloth, otherwise the new owner had to return it or pay a price fixed by the seller. Failing that, the seller was entitled to seize a man from the quarter of the buyer and sell him. If the price of the slave was fixed but not paid over and the slave died the seller had to bear the loss. If, however, any sum had been paid on account and the slave died, the buyer was the loser. The price of a slave at Isele Asaba was twenty bags for one in the prime of life, that is to say, between the age of 12 and 40. From the age of 40 upwards the price was fifteen bags, but old slaves were worth only ten bags.

At Ibuzǫ, on the other hand, the price was twenty bags, for an old slave it was thirteen bags, and forty for a young man or woman between the age of 20 and 30.

At Ezi the price was, in later times, twenty bags, and I was told by the old men that originally they paid no more than one or two bags. They were of course frequently used for burial and similar purposes.

Substitutes.—If a slave by dint of hard work could raise sufficient money to buy another slave to give to his owner, he was free from work. He was not, however, absolutely free, for his property at his death was his master's and his master was also responsible for his debts.

At Asaba, Qkpanam, Isele Asaba, Ala, Ibuzọ, Idumuje Uboko and Ezi a male slave could purchase a substitute in the way mentioned above and be free every day to work on his own farm.

At Onitsha Olona and Ubulubu the conditions were somewhat different. If a slave got money and purchased another slave he not only became free from work, but became absolutely a freed man. He joined the umunna of his master, and if he had a slave wife belonging to the same master, she and her children became free. If on the other hand he had married a slave woman belonging to another master she would-be sent back with her children.

At Oboluku, on the other hand, a slave who purchased a substitute still had to work for his master, if the statement made to me was correct.

At Ibuzọ a slave who purchased a substitute usually worked on afọ and ẹke for himself (the information was somewhat contradictory) but could be summoned by his master to work on afọ, especially if his master were an old man; but as a compensation for this the owner's children could help the slave on his farm.

A slave might purchase a substitute at Asaba, and in this case, though he was not free, he would only be called upon by his master when there was much work to do.

Marriage.—If a male slave wished to marry he could obtain a wife by purchase, that is to say, enter into a marriage of an ordinary type, differing only from the normal form, owing to the fact that he himself was not free. In this case, whether the wife was purchased by the master's money or the slave's own money, she remained a slave and became the property of her husband's owner. The children were, in this case, also slaves.

At Nsukwa, the same rule prevailed as in some parts of the Awka district, and the children of slaves were reckoned as free born.

As Asaba, the rule was that if a slave, who took a female slave to wife, gave more than one shilling's worth of palm wine to her owner, the woman was reckoned as his proper wife and the children followed the father. If an Onitsha female slave came to Asaba, not as a wife, but in the mbwa relationship (see p. 80), the owner of the father was entitled to take one child in payment of the board of the woman and her children. The male slave provided food for six months only, and the female slave for the remaining six months.

If a disobedient slave were sold, his wife would not necessarily be sold with him ; she might be given to another husband. It must, of course, be remembered that slaves would not often be sold except for misconduct, in fact, a good slave might almost be regarded as a child.

At Qkpanam, if the female slave belonged to another man, the children followed the mother, but the price of thirty bags, paid either by the slave or his master, would make the woman his wife ; that is to say, the ordinary purchase price of a slave. The purchase price of a female slave for the mbwa relationship was two bags, if more was paid the children belonged to the owner of the father.

At Isele Asaba, the owner could purchase a wife for his slave, or the slave could pay 140 cowries and become mbwa of a woman belonging to another master.

At Onitsha Olona, a female slave lived with her husband even if the relationship was only that of mbwa (p. 80), but she would sweep the house and get wood and water for her owner, and, if her owner were sick, she might even leave her husband to look after the patient. The slave husband offered to the mwǫ of the woman's owner. He might give one bag to the mother of the woman. The normal price of a slave wife was twenty bags, and, if she was purchased for this purpose

PLATE XI.

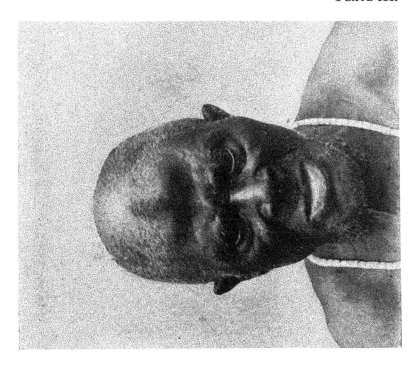

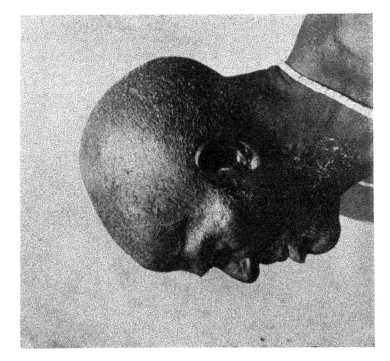

OLD MAN (IBUZO).

her status differed so far from that of other women purchased solely as slaves, that she could not be sold, at any rate apart from her husband. It appears that at Onitsha Olona a male slave might be called upon to do a certain amount of work for the owner of the female slave with whom he was in mbwa.

At Ibuzọ, the owner could purchase a wife for his slave or the slave himself could get an mbwa. In that case he had to pay one bag to bring her out of ukoni, the kitchen in which the food of men of certain status has to be cooked. If the husband wished to purchase her children, he could so at the ordinary rates.

At g ashi, when a man got a wife, the price being fifteen or twenty bags, he would do no more work on his owner's farm. If on the other hand he took an mbwa, according to one statement, the woman's owner would get any property that she gathered; on the other hand, she would not go to her owner to do work, though she might take wood.

At Obọmpa, a female slave had to give ifenru to her owner to worship his father. A slave had to work for the owner of his wife if it was an mbwa relationship. The slave husband could not buy a child from the owner of his wife.

At Ukunzu, the price of a female slave was three to five bags. The rule about the children was so far peculiar, that sons would work half their time for their owner, and half their time for their own father.

Dues.—It was a regular rule that slaves, both male and female, brought ifenru or dues to their owners, occasionally also to other people at such times as the New Yam Feast.

At Ọkpanam, the amount was fixed at ten yams, one vessel of palm wine and a certain amount of kola and one goat. Ten yams were also due to the ọkpala of the owner.

At Onitsha Olona a female slave sent a goat, fish and yams yearly to her owner; or according to another statement, one goat, one bag of cowries and yams. A male slave sent seven yams and kola. After a slave had tied his yams in his farm, the master got five ntoto out of ten abwẹli (p. 177), but if the slave had less than six, the master would take none.

I 2

At Ala, the yearly contribution was five yams, one ngugu and palm wine. This was due also to the owner of his wife. After tying his yams, the slave gave twenty mbubwa (p. 177) to his owner. If, on the other hand, the slave did not raise many yams, the owner might take one mbubwa only.

At Ibuzọ, after tying his yams, the slave might retain all at his owner's pleasure, or else give one mbubwa, fourteen big yams known as Ji ọnọmụz' irhe (the yams at the gate of irhe).

At Obuluku, the yams grown on the slave's farm were his master's, and the division of them depended upon the will of the master; there was no fixed proportion. He would, however, assure himself that the yams left in the slave's possession were properly used, that is to say, either for food or the purchase of live stock.

At Idumuje Uboko a male slave gave five yams to his owner and one calabash of palm wine with which to worship his father. The yams were shared equally. The female slave gave one goat to her owner or 5s., and could also make cloth for him.

Property.—Under ordinary circumstances the master was the owner of the whole of the slave's property. It has, however, already been mentioned that at Onitsha Olona a slave could purchase his freedom with his own earnings. An exception to the ordinary rule that a slave's earnings on his own days are his property is made by a regulation found at Ukunzu, that if a slave hunted on ẹke day, the game belonged to his master.

At Ọkpanam, a slave would work on his owner's farm every day, but would work on his own farm till the owner came, but any property thus earned, though he had the use of it during his lifetime, passed to his owner at death, as also did any money which his master gave him in lieu of free days. In practice, it probably happened, as a rule, that the son of a slave inherited his property, and the slave husband inherited the wife's property.

At Asaba, however, I was told that the owner could not

force the son of his slave to hand over any of his father's property. Gifts made by the female slave to her husband or her mbwa with the consent of her owner became his property.

At O ọ pa, a female slave could give property to her husband or her mbwa. In the latter case it could not be claimed at her death provided she had informed her owner at the time. It was, in every case, essential that the slaves should keep their owners duly informed of any property they acquired.

Civil Rights.—A slave would often retain civil rights in his own country. At Isele Asaba, for example, it was held that if a slave returned he could recover his house and land. His wife could even follow him into slavery with her children and retain her freedom.

At Obọmpa it was held that a slave could become dibia (doctor) in another town, though a two-third share of his earnings went to his owner as long as he remained a slave.

At Onitsha Olona if the eldest son of a man was a slave at his father's death the second son would take charge, but if the brother returned he would hand over the property. The titles made by a man who fell into slavery would not be extinguished, but the shares payable to him (see p. 54) would be the property of the second brother until the slave regained his freedom.

Freeing Male Slaves.—It was in most cases possible to free both male and female slaves. In the latter case the object was usually marriage, though in certain towns this seems to have been forbidden. It must be remembered that some of the slaves, at any rate, were prisoners of war, and in this case men and women were treated differently. At Onitsha Olona the males were sold and the females kept as wives. The captor could give her to his son but could not dispose of her otherwise. At Oboluku a captive of war was sent to the obi but could not be sold; for his town would redeem him at the end of the war if not too many people had been killed by his town of origin. If the slaughter had been too great he might be retained as a slave.

The feeling about freeing slaves seems to have differed in different places. At Asaba, apparently, a slave was looked upon more in the light of property. I was told that though an owner had the right to free his slaves and could allow them to be redeemed by their own people at the price of two slaves, he would not think of setting them free at his own motion, for this would inflict an injury on his heirs.

At Ǫkpanam, on the other hand, it was held that a man could set a male slave free and adopt him as his son. They never took captives in war according to their statement, but got their slaves from the Ụzibwo, or Road of Slaves (Igbo or Ibo), that is to say, the other side of the Niger.

At Isele Asaba, where a good slave was regarded as a child and buried behind the owner's či, he might be set free. The owner informed the ǫkpalẹbo, who called the ẹbo together at his house. Three bags of cowries were there shared among the ẹbo and the slave was accounted one of them. If anyone, therefore, called him slave again, a fine of three bags and one goat was paid to the ǫkpalẹbo by the offender. A slave thus set free could marry a free woman and take a title. Like the son of an idẹbwe he could not become ǫkpala.

At Onitsha Olona a male slave could be set free by offering to the mwǫ in the house of the ǫkpalẹbo. My informants said that there was no way of setting a female slave free, nor yet could the son of a slave be freed, but these statements were not subsequently supported. Here, as at Isele Asaba, a freed slave, whether set free by his master or, as before noticed, by a process of self-redemption, could marry a free woman and take a title. If a freed slave had a slave wife she became free with her children, provided she belonged to the same master. If she belonged to another master her husband had to redeem her. Children by another slave belonging to the same master were set free with their mother.

At Ala a male slave was never set free, and a female slave only if the owner proposed to marry her.

At Ibuzọ the father of a female slave who was set free could also be freed, and with him all his children acquire free status. I was told that all slaves were bought, and that prisoners of war went back to their own country at the end of the war. If they chose they could marry and even become members of the community.

At Idumuje Uboko, I was told that slaves were never set free. At Ukunzu male slaves might be set free and adopted if a man had no sons, and the blood brother of a female slave, set free in order that the owner might marry her, likewise became free if they were under the same master.

At O ọ pa if a man of the same ẹbo became či (see p. 19) to a female slave's child, the owner might set the child free by calling the ẹbo together and sacrificing a goat to the mwọ. A free man might marry a girl who was set free, but her change in status did not affect that of her brothers and sisters.

At Ubulubu the status of a slave seems to have differed somewhat from that which was customary in other places. Not only could a slave give a slave to his owner and become free, as was the case at Onitsha Olona and Ubulubu, but even if he remained a slave he was buried in the house of his owner like a freeborn man; his ikẹṅga was put on the big ukbo and the grave alongside. On the other hand, a slave set free by killing a goat had to marry a slave or a freed slave, unless the idumu was decreasing in numbers, in which case he might be permitted to marry a free woman and take a title.

Guardians.—An old male slave might be guardian to his master's young son, and one informant said that he could address the women married into the ẹbo in exactly the same way as a free man. One case was cited to me in which a man, Obano by name, gave both his daughters to slaves for whom he could not afford to purchase slave wives. The umunna were called and 140 cowries, palm wine, five yams and kola were brought. The heads of the two women and the two slaves were touched with kola, which was then offered to Obano's father. This meant that the slaves were set free and became members of the ẹbo. The slave husband had to cleanse his body with a chicken and offer a goat on the ọfọ of the ẹbo before the assembled ẹbo, but this did not seem to be an essential part of the ceremony, as my informant said that he could keep his wife even if no goat were sacrificed. It seems clear that they actually married their owner's daughters, although one informant said that they did not; for another and better informed inhabitant of the town gave the names both of the women and of their husbands, and added that their children worshipped Obano instead of their actual fathers.

Another case that was cited to me was that of a slave Oke, who married a free woman, Idia, at Ukbeli. Her father claimed all the children and took them away, but by the order of a doctor they still come to worship Oke their father.

At Asaba a childless man could buy a slave to help him work his farm, and in this case the slave would help his master's brother with the funeral ceremonies when his master died. A slave might also act as guardian if the heir were small when the owner died, and in this case when he child grew up he would regard the slave as his father.

At Okpanam a slave might be the guardian of a boy, and would take him to live with him in his own house. When the boy grew up and took over the father's property, including the slave, the latter would not be required to do more than one day's work in the week.

A slave set free by his owner on his deathbed by the sacrifice of a goat was, apparently, in all respects like a free man, for he was considered to have been adopted by his owner, who only performed this ceremony if he had no children of his own.

At Ezi a male slave could be set free and could then marry a free woman.

At Nsukwa, where the status of a slave was so far different from that of other places in the district that his children were free, a man might likewise purchase a slave and adopt him as his son. In this case the owner touched the slave's forehead with kola in the presence of his family and declared that he adopted him because he had no son, at the same time begging the mwǫ not to let his child die. The adopted son took all his owner's property.

Freeing Female Slaves.—At Asaba according to my information a man could not take a slave woman as his wife.

At Ǫkpanam a man could marry his female slave. All the ębo met in the ǫkpalębo's house and the suitor gave the girl another name, sacrificed a goat and declared that she was now free. It was forbidden to marry a slave' in the same idumu or the same ębo, nor might a man marry one of his father's slaves (presumably in his father's lifetime) nor yet a slave belonging to his mother's family.

At Isele Asaba I was told that they never married a slave woman.

At Onitsha Olona a man might marry a female slave by offering a goat in the ǫkpalębo's house to the mwǫ. He could not, however, marry the daughter of one of his own slaves. Here, unlike other places, a female slave was able to free herself, and her change in status meant that all her children also became free.

At Ala a man might set a female slave free in order to marry her. This was done as soon as he purchased her by sacrificing a goat in the house of the ǫkpalębo. Thereafter anyone who called the woman a slave paid a fine of a goat.

At Ibuzǫ two goats were provided by a man who wished to marry a female slave, which were sacrificed to the oke ani, to the ani and to the ndičie of the husband. If anyone called her "slave" after this ceremony the fine was four goats. It appears that at Ibuzǫ a man might marry the daughter of his own slave if her mother were the property of another owner.

At Oboluku a man might buy a slave in order to marry

her. The owner announced the fact to the u m u n n a and the idumu and the suitor called his own umunna and took a goat to meet the others, and then the owner offered the goat to the mwọ and declared that the slave was free and the suitor paid the price. The suitor could also buy a woman and set her free or set free an already owned slave.

At Idumuje Uboko slaves were not set free for the purpose of marriage.

At Ukunzu a man could not marry the daughter of his slave nor adopt her until she was set free. He could, however, buy a female slave and at the same time take her to wife without further ceremony. No one could call her slave after her marriage, and her children were in the same position as the children of a free-born woman.

At O ọ pa a man could set a woman free in order to marry her and then all her children would be free. She could not, however, marry her owner nor a man of the same ẹbo.

At Ezi a man could free the daughter of a female slave by sacrificing a goat in the presence of the ẹbo and take her to wife. The rest of her family remained slaves.

At Nsukwa a man could marry a female slave without ceremony.

Ownership and Inheritance of Slaves.—The ordinary rule was that slaves, like the house, went to the eldest son, though in the section on inheritance it is shown that, where a man died possessed of many slaves, other sons besides the eldest could receive one. An owner would build a house for a female slave and feed her, but a male slave, unless he were a young boy, would undertake the work for himself. Where children were born to a slave husband and wife belonging to different owners, the children would remain with the wife until they were old enough, and then go to their proper owner's house. The rule that the eldest son was heir to the slaves held good even if the slave were given to a wife.

At g ashi a woman could own slaves bought with her money. She would ask her husband's advice and he would strike the bargain and pay over the money. At her husband's death they would become his property.

Runaways.—In comparatively thickly populated districts like Asaba it was not difficult for a slave to run from his master. Where the population was scantier it was equally possible for him to escape; for, some 50 years ago, forest appears to have occupied a much larger area than it does at the present. There were well understood rules as to the methods of dealing with runaway slaves. If a slave ran at Asaba money would be paid if he fled to a friendly town. If his hosts were hostile he would go to another master, who beat a drum and rejoiced. If he ran to his own town he might be free if he had people to stand by him, otherwise he might be sold again by the original sellers.

At Isele Asaba a runaway slave was called ǫsǫ́; the man to whom he ran was called ebo; he offered drink to his friends and fired a gun, saying that a slave had run to him. If a man found a slave on the road he killed a goat to be eaten by all the ębo, and the slave himself got the head. The master would shave the head of his slave before his ikęṅga, and then pour oil upon his ikęṅga, and give his slave a new cloth exactly as though he had purchased him. My informants thought that the shaving of the hair was to show that the man was a slave. After this ceremony the slave was led to the ǫkpalębo and then to the Ẹzeṅwani or head chief.

At Onitsha Olona a runaway slave might be taken to Iyase, who would take him to the head chief. Iyase would then be ordered to sell the slave; half the price went to the finder and half to the rest of the town. A state of hostilities, however, between the town to which the slave ran, and Onitsha Olona itself, did not prevent the owner from asking for the slave; he would do so, and if the captor refused to hand the slave over the owner might seize a person. In any case no payment would be made. If a small boy found a slave and took him home, the slave might be declared to be the boy's property, and the father would hold him for him.

At Ibuzọ the finder of a runaway slave called his umunna and rejoiced. If the owner claimed the slave, he had to bring a big goat, a fish known as mbuazu and palm wine for the finder. The obligation to restore slaves was reciprocal. If Asaba, for example, failed to restore Ibuzọ's slaves, Ibuzọ would do the like. It was held that a slave who managed to return to his own country was free. A runaway slave would often hide in the bush and attach himself to a man whom he liked.

At g ashi a runaway slave was never sent back, but handed to Iyase, who took him to the Obi.

At Oboluku, if a slave ran to his previous owner, the latter could be forced to pay the price to the loser. A runaway slave, who was here called odido, was taken to obi, who gave a goat, 5s. and cloth to the value of 5s. to the man who brought him. The obi might demand ten or twenty bags for restoring him to the owner.

At Idumuje Uboko a runaway was never kept. The owner would pay a certain sum to recover him. Apparently there was an objection felt to receiving slaves as a part of the community, for my informants added that only free people ran to Idumuje to stop.

At Ukunzu the owner followed a runaway slave and claimed him, fortifying his claim by the payment of one to five bags. If the slave were not handed over the umunna of the owner would help him to seize a person.

At Ezi a runaway slave who went to a house became the property of the owner of the house. One found on the road was handed to the head chief and sold, but the purchaser would be a stranger and not an inhabitant of Ezi. One share went to the obi, one to the ikei ani and one to the finder.

At Nsukwa the owner might ask for the restoration of a runaway slave, or the slave might remain away on condition of paying an annual tribute of yams.

In certain towns like Oboluku and Isẹluku there was a special quarter devoted to slaves, but in the former case only the obi's slaves inhabited it. They were called Ibiagwali and properly speaking belonged to no quarter, and are still in this condition in the present day.

Theft.—If a slave stole from anyone but his owner he might be seized by the loser or his price claimed from the owner.

At Qkpanam, if the loser were of the same i d u m u he would speak to the owner and warn him, if of another i d u m u, he would hold the owner responsible. If the owner were an ẹze the fine would be ten bags and one goat. The goat was sacrificed on the Nze (p. 51) which was usually kept in the u k o n i or cooking place. In the case of less important people the money only was payable. An habitual thief, however, would be sold and they would remark " His money (*i.e.* his purchase money) will not choke him," but of course well behaved slaves were not sold unless a purchaser came who wished to make a slave woman his wife.

At Onitsha Olona a slave who stole anything would be flogged and sold at the third offence. If he stole from other slaves, application would be made to his master, but he would be seized if he stole from a free man.

At Obuluku a thief was held for redemption and if no money were forthcoming he would be pawned, but if the thief ran the owner could not be held responsible.

At Ukunzu a slave's money was taken to pay his fine but his owner was liable to make up the amount if funds were insufficient.

At Isele Asaba if a slave stole from a free man or a slave, one bag was the fine, unless the second slave belonged to the same owner. A slave who stole from his owner was punished by his owner and might be sold.

Murder.—The responsibility of the owner of a slave who committed murder was at least as great as that of the owner of a dishonest slave. According to one Qkpanam informant the owner had to give his daughter to the brother of the murdered man, if he were a free man, or be himself hanged; but this was denied by others. If the murdered man was a slave the offender would be hanged. Another account said that if a slave murdered a free man he would be taken to bury him and the owner gave his daughter. A slave was hanged for the murder of a slave and if he ran the owner bought a slave as a substitute. This he was free to do in any case if, for any reason, he did not wish to lose his slave. The rule was the same whether the slave was a man or woman.

At Isele Asaba the customs were the same but a slave who killed a slave might be given in his place. If both slaves belonged to one master the murderer would be sold by his owner.

At Onitsha Olona a slave was hanged for the murder of a slave, but the owner of the murdered man had no redress.

At Ala, on the other hand, the owner was liable to pay compensation for the murder of a slave. For the murder of a free man a woman also had to be handed over or his owner might be hanged.

At Oboluku a slave was hanged for the murder of a free man or slave.

At Obọmpa I was told that according to hearsay the owner of a slave might be hanged if the slave killed a free man, but they had never seen an instance. A slave might be hanged for the murder of a slave or might be handed over in place of the murdered man.

At Ezi, on the other hand, a slave was not hanged for the murder of a free man but his owner took his place unless he was prepared to pay compensation in the ordinary way.

VII.—CIVIL LAW.

INHERITANCE.—The custom of inheritance in the Asaba district is that which is commonly found in the Ibo country. The first-born son is heir to the property, but if there is more than one wife the eldest sons of other wives may receive a larger or smaller share, which, however, in some cases is only the bride price of their own sisters of the whole blood.

It must be remembered in dealing with these questions that the eldest son is not necessarily the son of the head wife, any more than the head wife is necessarily the woman for whom a man has first begun to pay bride price. Properly speaking, the definition of first wife is that she is the wife who first cooks for a man ; this at any rate was the definition at Ubulubu. In Asaba of course the Auase or Isimwọ custom further complicates the question (see p. 62). Again the first-born son is the son actually the oldest by birth, not the son of the first wife. In a case which came under my notice at Onitsha Ubwo the first-born son was the child of the third wife.

The first-born son takes the place of his father. His brothers come to him for advice and ask his permission to marry. The daughters, if adult, bring their suitors before him, and the suitors of small daughters make their first application to him ; if he objects to the suitor, the suitor will be rejected ; if he accepts him a present of kola is due to him. If the other children of his father are small he keeps them in his own house. They work for him and he provides food for them, and when the males reach manhood, if his means allow it, he pays the bride price of their wives. In Asaba, if the children are too numerous he can send them to their mother's people. Anything which is done for half-sisters is without prejudice to the right of the brother of the whole blood to the bride price of such sisters.

The eldest son is, in Asaba, the natural heir to all the widows save his own mother. The women, however, may refuse and go either to one of the brothers or to one of the umunna, under ordinary circumstances the widow is entitled to if'ubwo or plants which she cultivates, or has cultivated for her in a portion of her husband's farm.

At Isele Asaba when the father dies the eldest son takes over the house, the other sons clear the bush round it and if there is space build their own houses. The younger sons actually reside in the house of the first-born, but, whether they reside or not, all the sons serve the first-born, that is to say they work on his farm, rebuild or repair his house and offer the customary portions of any game that they may kill, that is to say, one leg and part of the liver. When the young children grow up the first-born shows them where they can build their houses. Ordinarily a boy will build a small house for himself, a so-called bachelor's house, before he gets a wife. In this case his mother, if she is alive, will cook for him ; if not, the wife of the first born. The widows go to the eldest son, save, firstly, that he does not take his own mother to wife, and secondly, that any widow related to his own mother goes likewise to another son.

It may be noted in passing that if a man removes to his mother's country, he must reside near his mother's brother ; he does not become the owner of land but has only the use of it ; though anything that he plants, such as kola, kokonut, etc., is his own. He does not, however, enjoy full civil rights, for, exactly like the son of an idębwe, he cannot become
ǫkpala.

At Ibuzǫ, Ala and Ǫkpanam the heir is the eldest son. At g ashi, on the other hand, this is only true if the first-born actually buries his father. In either case the other sons are entitled to a small share.

In one case that came under my notice the first-born took the obu bead as a matter of right, and was heir to the house ; he took one slave, all the boxes, all the goats and all the trees. All the widows but one became his property ; the exception was not his own mother, who was dead. The second son got one slave and the third and fourth sons took one bead each.

In the case of another family the first-born took all the property, with the following exceptions : Three sons got one slave and one widow each, another got one slave, and two young boys got a cow each.

At Oboluku, on the other hand, the first-born son is the sole heir; failing a son, a brother, and if there is no brother, one of the umunna who buries him, probably the ǫkpala.

At Idumuje Uboko the first-born son is the heir but, as will be seen later, under certain conditions shares may go to the other sons.

At Ukunzu the rule with regard to widows is slightly different, for they stay in the house and get a friend outside; if they go to the sons, each son will get one so far as they last.

At Ezi about one third of the widows go to the first-born, and the others choose in succession. Two thirds of the slaves go to the first-born, and one each to the eldest sons of the other wives. In the case of a man who had several cows, three would go to the first-born, and the rest singly to such sons as were entitled to slaves but did not get them.

At Nsukwa the first-born gets a big share, and the eldest sons of each wife get smaller shares.

At Onitsha Olona the house of the widow appears to be broken down, but my information is not quite clear, for in the case that came under my notice the house was in a bad state and uninhabitable. The son broke it down and' rebuilt it for his wife.

A case at Ubulubu was somewhat remarkable for the fact that the heir married a stepdaughter of his father. According to a statement made to me, the second son inherited his father's property, although his elder brother, who was dead, had left three sons, one of whom has now succeeded to the property of his dead uncle. The family was a large one and in the genealogy, as actually recorded, the mother of

Nwokonta, the actual heir, appears as the second wife. It appears probable, however, that this is simply due to the fact that my informants, as commonly happens, placed their mother in the position of first wife. At any rate, Nwokonta took the bride price of the only half-sister who was unmarried at his father's death.

At Obọmpa, if a man has no child his ṅwago may bury him and take his property to the exclusion of his brother. If there is more than one ṅwago the older is the heir.

Idebwe.—The customs of inheritance are, however, modified in the Asaba district, firstly, by the Idẹbwe custom, and secondly, by women marrying women. In the first case the idẹbwe herself is the heir, provided there are no sons. At Nsukwa, if one wife out of several bears daughters only and the others bear sons, one or more, one daughter of the former could be made idẹbwe and take her share with the sons.

Under ordinary circumstances the idẹbwe seems to be put in the place of a man, and though I did not investigate many specific cases, it seems certain that she inherits her father's house, or, at any rate, holds the house and other property in trust for her children. Under certain circumstances her father's brother may be her heir, but this would equally be the case if the idẹbwe were a man similarly placed.

At Ubulubu more than one interesting case came under my notice, doubtless owing to the fact that it is a border town, and therefore more affected by Ishan customs. In one case a woman, who had gone over the border to Emule, left her husband because he was bad, and earned money by trading while she was living in her brother's house. Her eldest brother inherited her property; as the woman was not living with her husband she was unable to take a wife (see p. 83). She, however, purchased a wife for her brother, apparently with the idea of making the children of this wife her heirs, but no children were born. She also engaged a wife at Emule, but the money for her was earned in her husband's house, and the woman was taken by one of her husband's brothers. The situation was further complicated by the fact that her husband paid only 5s. as bride price for her in order that he and her father might share her children. No children, however, were born.

At Ukunzu, if a daughter is idẹbwe, though she gets the cooking things mentioned above as coming to a daughter who has not gone to her husband, she would only have the use of beads or cloth.

At Obọmpa, in a case which came under my notice, the house does not appear to have gone to the idẹbwc, as her brother is stated to have taken charge of it, and he is also reckoned as the father of her son. As the idẹbwe, however, is dead, and before her death appears to have married a husband, the inference may be wrong.

In a certain number of cases the woman is really in the position of an idẹbwe without actual necessity. In a case that came under my notice in Ubulubu, a man who had carried out the preliminaries of marriage was unable to complete payment of the price, and never took his wife from her father's house. Apparently the relationship went on for some 20 years at least, as the woman was 40 when her husband died. Only one child was born, a boy, and he was reckoned as the property of his maternal grandfather, and inherited some of his property, although one of his mother's brothers is still alive and has six sons. In another idẹbwe case at Ubulubu the idẹbwe was the eldest of the family. She had one half-brother, Badi, alive, who has now five wives, but the idẹbwe and Badi shared the property, one kokonut tree going to Omona, the younger brother of Badi, since dead. The case is also interesting from the point of view of the ordinary law of inheritance, inasmuch as the mother of the idẹbwe went to Badi and Badi's mother went to a brother of his father's who had helped to bury his father. The third wife of the father may have been already dead, as she was the widow of the grandfather.

Gifts.—The customs are modified in another direction, not directly by testamentary dispositions, but by gifts within the lifetime. Thus, at Asaba, a man at the point of death can give gifts to any of his sons in the presence of his male children and of the elders of the family. At Ala a man can make gifts to any of his sons ; the first-born would be present but cannot hinder the gift. If, however, a man has no sons, the brother can restrain him from disposing of his property otherwise.

At g ashi, if a father has a favourite son, he can give some of his property to him in the presence of the first-born. When he does so he must also give kola to the son and repeat words to the effect that the property will not hurt him. This can be done either when the man is on his deathbed or at any previous time.

At Oboluku a man can make gifts to his second or any other son, and this whether he is sick or well. He calls his own brother and his eldest son to witness. In making gifts he strikes his ǫfǫ on the ground and tells the recipient that the gift is not to injure him. If he has no children of his own the gift can be made to his sister's child, and may include the whole of his property.

At Idumuje Uboko gifts of this kind are recognised only if the donor is at the point of death, or at least in bad health.

At Ubulubu gifts can be made by the father either at the point of death or when he is in his ordinary health, and the same rule is found at Ezi.

Bride Price.—The rule of inheritance as to the bride price usually differs from that which governs the disposition of other property. At Asaba the first-born son gets the price of all sisters by his own mother and of one daughter of each of the other wives. The price of the other daughters goes to their eldest blood brother in each case.

At Isele Asaba, on the other hand, the eldest son gets the price of all the daughters, and one goat only is paid to the brother of the full blood.

At Okpanam the price of the eldest half-sister in each family goes to the first-born, and he is bound to purchase a wife for the full brother of such half-sister.

At Ala the bride price goes to the eldest son, and the girl's own brother gets one bag of cowries.

At g ashi the eldest son, if he has three half-sisters by another mother, may take the price of two of them, and their own brother would take that of the remaining one. Where a woman bears only daughters the first-born son takes them all. Conversely, if a woman bears only sons the first-born obtains wives for them as far as his means allow. Where there are both sons and daughters the first-born does not obtain wives for such sons as receive the bride price of a sister.

At Oboluku the first-born gets the price of all daughters by all wives, but each blood brother, however many there may be of them, receives one goat from the suitor. If, therefore, the girl is a sister of the whole blood, the first-born son receives two cows and one goat. He also receives five bags of cowries (25s.) which is due to the one who has the girl in ǫma (see p. 51).

At Onitsha Olona the eldest son is the heir and takes the bride price of all his half-sisters.

At Obǫmpa the first-born gets the whole of the bride price for the sisters and half-sisters. As a set off against this he pays half the price of a wife of any of his brothers, or, failing that, he can assign to the brother the whole of the price of one of his own sisters.

At Onitsha Ubwo the first-born son gets the price of all half-sisters and purchases a wife for each of his half-brothers. He should also make titles for all the sons, who would, in their turn, send him yams from their farms, or a portion of the money that they gained by trading or in any other ways. If the first-born son fails to do his duty this contribution would not be paid, and it appears that sons who had begun to pay them, in consideration of favours received, might stop them in retaliation for failure to carry out the obligations towards their younger brothers or half-brothers.

Guardians.—As usually happens, the father's brother is the guardian of any heir or heirs who are too small to look after the property for themselves. At Asaba the idumu can make representations, apparently, if he misappropriates the property, but can do nothing further to restrain him. When, however, the child is of age he can claim the property which is his due. The heir would summon, firstly, his mother's people, calling upon the guardian to do the same, and secondly, his idumu. The old people would be called upon to give evidence, and capable men, six or more, would be appointed to try the case.

At Onitsha Olona the guardian is the brother or half-brother of the father. Yams and perishable produce he could sell and keep the money for himself, and the increase of live stock is his also. He can use money as he pleases but at the proper time must be prepared to hand over the right amount, which will be known to the members of his ẹbo. If the guardian does not account for the money he can be reported and the ẹbo will call upon him to hand it over; at the same time it does not seem to be regarded precisely as a debt that he owes to his nephew. The guardian takes all the adult wives, and the boy must be able to keep both himself and a wife before he takes over the property. If the boy is a minor and his father had engaged wives who had, however, not finally gone to live with him, such wives may be given by the guardian to a friend until such time as the heir reaches manhood. They would live in the guardian's house and he would care for them and their children, in respect of whose keep he is not entitled to make any charge; the children would, of course, be the property of the heir. If however, the heir should die, his father's brother might take her from the friend who, it may be noted, would be of another ẹbo. If a man from the same ẹbo should cohabit with her, a goat should be killed or, according to native belief, she would not conceive any children. During the minority of the heir the bride price of girls would go to the guardian. It would fall upon him to engage wives for the heir, but he could also utilise the bride price to secure wives for himself.

At Ala the guardian keeps the wives and children of the

dead man until the heir is adult; a wife may be given to a friend if she is old enough. Yams may be sold and the money kept by the guardian, but stock and produce all go to the heir. If the guardian is suspected of embezzlement, the son, or anyone else in the ẹbo, can complain to the ọkpalẹbo and the ẹbo would call upon the guardian to make restitution.

At Ibuzọ the guardian will take one slave for himself and give one to the son, and live stock would be similarly treated; but if five cows out of ten went to the son, the remaining five must be used by the guardian to buy nkpese and alo titles for the heir, if necessary. The guardian would also utilise property of this sort in payment of debts. A careless or unfaithful guardian can be warned by the umunna. It may be noted that at Ibuzọ a half-brother of the father may be the heir or the guardian, if full brothers are too young.

At. g ashi the guardian may utilise some of the property to bring up the children and must obtain wives for the sons, as many as he can. If, however, they see him embezzling or wasting the property they are powerless, though in theory he should hand over all that is not otherwise accounted for.

At Oboluku a greater amount of control exists over the guardian. If he were seen to be embezzling the property the head of the umunna would call on the ike ani, and the oldest man in the town would warn him; if necessary he could be replaced. Perishable property would be sold, but all stock and produce belong to the heir. On handing over the property the guardian is called upon to take an oath in the presence of the head of the ẹbo.

At Ukunzu both stock and produce have to be handed over, and also any money from the sale of goods. If the guardian embezzles, the family of the heir's mother and his own umunna will warn him. It is believed that the ọfọ of the heir's father will kill him, if he goes too far in this direction.

At Ubulubu the guardian is always the one who buried the father. A certain number of the widows will become his property; others are handed to friends till the sons of the dead man are old enough.

Occasionally the mother may be the guardian. At O ǫ pa a case of this sort came under my notice. After marrying a wife a man died, leaving a young son, whose mother married his uncle and became his guardian. The property was handed over when the ward was about 20.

In a case at Ukunzu where the daughter of an idębwe, Ekusi, became the wife (p. 83) of a childless woman, the wife of Okoma, Osagiana the son of Okoma, became guardian to Ekusi's child. Whether this was the ordinary rule or not it was difficult to discover, for Ekusi was of the same ǫbo as Okoma. Had she not been, she would have married him or one of his sons. Native custom was, however, disregarded, and the court handed her to Osagiana, whereas she ought to have remained with her mbwa in charge of Okoma. The situation was further complicated by the fact that her first mbwa left her because he wished to take a doctor's title, and decided to travel.

Strangers.—It probably happened comparatively rarely in olden times that a man left his own country and died in a strange land. Such cases as happened were of more frequent occurrence on the banks of the Niger than inland, and at Ala it was laid down that the host of a stranger should keep his property till his people came to claim it. Before their arrival he was not entitled to pay the dead man's debts, unless he were a witness at the time the debt was incurred. It is of course incumbent on a host to enquire of a guest, as soon as he arrives, as to his place of origin and his kinsmen.

WOMAN'S PROPERTY.—It was pointed out in the report on the Awka district* that the conceptions with regard to woman's property were on the whole vague, and, broadly

---

PLATE XII.

YOUNG **MAN OF** ASABA WITH **OZELE** HAIR.

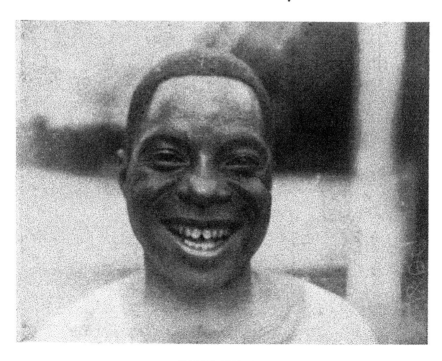

TOOTH-FILING.

speaking, the same is true of the Asaba district, though here there are, on the whole, fewer contradictions and, perhaps, more real differences in customs from town to town.

In Asaba I was told that the whole of a woman's property belongs to her husband, and that she must even tell her husband before she takes her own money to spend. The husband may, in case of need, borrow money from his wife in her absence, but he must tell her on her return, and will have to pay back, unless it was for the benefit of her own child. If these statements correctly represent the native view it is obvious that the woman's property is not, as I have said, the property of the husband, but the joint property of husband and wife, and that the consent of both is needed before it can be expended, unless, indeed, the view be taken that the husband is required to repay his loan, not because his wife has any claim upon the money, but because it is really the property of the child.

If a wife is dismissed by her husband, or runs away, she can take nothing; even the cloth that she wears must be paid for, and is included in the sum mentioned as due on account of the bride price. When a man dies the cotton and koko yams which a widow has planted are regarded as her own (generally speaking, of the farm produce the heir takes only the yams and leaves the if'ubwo (p. 61) for the widows).

At Onitsha Olona, if a wife runs away, it is held that she can take no property with her ; even what she trades with is the property of her husband, if he gave her the capital to start trading with; if she attempts to take it, it is theft. Even if her parents give her capital, her child is the lawful owner of it, and, in the absence of a child, her husband or his heir.

As at Asaba each woman is held to own what she has planted in the farm. At Ala the rule stated was somewhat different. A woman keeps what she gains, but it belongs to her husband and he can get it, though only by personal application to his wife, for any purpose that he likes to use it for. If she runs away he can claim it from her umunna. If, on the other hand, the husband drives his wife away, she can take with her the whole of her property, money, cloth, ivory, etc. This difference in the law relating to woman's property corresponds to a difference in the law of ownership of children. For it is held in Ebu and Ala that if a husband drives his wife out she can return to her umunna with her children, and a case actually came under my notice in which a woman's umunna refused to receive her, because she did not bring all her children with her. The law at Ala, therefore, bears out the theory that a woman's property may be regarded as legally owned by her children.

At Ibuzọ another slightly different statement was given me. A woman who trades in the market does not own her property, but, on the other hand, her husband cannot compel her to bring it to him for his own use. A wife, however, who leaves her husband, or is driven out, can take nothing, though it would not be accounted precisely as stealing, for the wife would not be punished, though one of her kin might be seized to secure the return of the property.

At g ashi I was told that a husband can take his wife's property without informing her, and if she leaves her husband for any reason he takes all her property; this is even the case when the ọmu leaves her husband; he takes all her property and uses it as he pleases. A woman who runs from her husband, if she goes to live in her father's house and the price is not repaid, has no property; her husband owns all; if the price is repaid her brother owns her property.

At Ubulubu it is held that what a woman gets in her husband's house is her husband's; what she owned before she came to her husband is her son's, and failing a son her husband can claim it, even if the bride price has been repaid. If a husband sends a wife away she can take with her what she brought and what she got in his house, unless she has a son. A son keeps all the property as his own.

PLATE XIII.

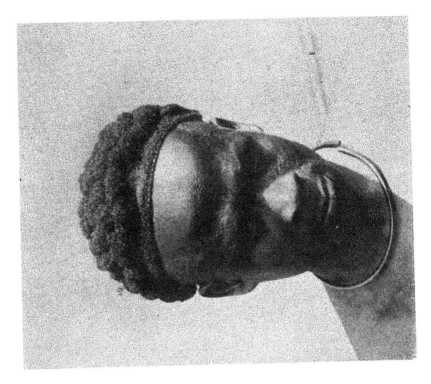

YOUNG MAN (ASABA) WITH ISI KPOLOKPOLO.

OFOME, OF OBOLUKU, WHO BORE EIGHT CHILDREN BEFORE
MAN OF 55 WAS BORN.

If she is sent to o bi she takes no property; it all belongs to her husband.

I did not find a case which precisely bore out these statements; in an analogous instance the matter was complicated by the fact that the parties to the case lived one on each side of the border. A woman of Ubulubu married into the Ishan country and left her husband because he was a bad man. Her brother inherited what she earned by trading after her return and also a wife whom his sister engaged for him. It was held that this wife could not be claimed by the husband of the woman or his people because the money for the bride price was earned in Ubulubu. A second wife, on the other hand, whom she had engaged at Emule in the Ishan country went to her husband's brother, her husband being already dead, because she had earned the money to pay for her in her husband's house. As mentioned, however, under Inheritance, the matter was further complicated by the fact that the bride price paid for the woman whose property was in question was only 5s. How far this affected the native view of the case it was difficult to ascertain, but from the fact that the husband's brother claimed one of the wives it appeared that the ordinary view of woman's property prevailed.

At Onitsha Ubwo a husband cannot take his wife's property without telling her, but he may borrow it. He is, however, under obligation to repay it unless she has expressly made a gift of it. If a woman runs from her husband she may take nothing with her if she has any children; if, on the other hand, she has no child she can take with her all that she has. If a woman goes to her father's house leaving children behind, nothing that she gains in her father's house passes to her child. I did not ascertain what would happen if she married another husband, in which case her father is said to receive a price, and not her first husband; but it was stated that if she leaves her husband on account of a quarrel and has no child, her brother is her heir.

At Idumuje Ụnọ a much more drastic view of a husband's

rights prevails. The husband provides the capital for trading and therefore owns it. What she brings from her parents is her husband's property, because he has earned it by doing service to her parents. If a husband takes his wife's money in her absence and refuses to repay, the only reply that she would get if she began a quarrel with him would be, " Whoever owns you, owns the money, and I won't pay."

At Ukunzu likewise a husband is at liberty to take his wife's money, but here the husband and wife are so far on equal terms that it is held permissible for a wife to take her husband's money in his absence. In neither case is there any obligation to repay. It appears to be a rare thing for a husband to dismiss his wife.

At Obọmpa if a woman has money the husband can take it, but if they are on bad terms he will repay it, which seems to set a premium on quarrelling. If she leaves her husband, or is turned out by him, she can take nothing, even though she be childless.

At Nsukwa the husband owns the property of a woman trader, but the rules with regard to women not under the protection of a husband are wholly different from those which are found elsewhere. If a woman is living in her husband's house her property is her father's, whether she be idẹbwe or not, but a friend may beg her for assistance and receive it. After the death of her father she owns herself and keeps her own money. If she dies childless, the ọkpala of her umunna takes the property. If a husband dismisses his wife she may take pots, cloth, and other ordinary property, but not money. Ornaments, such as ivory anklets, remain with the husband unless they are actually being worn.

Inheritance.—The rules for the disposition of a dead woman's property are somewhat more complex than in the ease of a man. At Asaba the heir was her eldest son, and she might make gifts to others in the presence of the heir. She was, however, limited with regard to these gifts, for costly things could not be disposed of in this way, only cooking pots, ordinary beads, cloth, and the like. If she had no children her husband was the next heir, failing him her husband's eldest son, and if she had neither husband nor stepsons her brothers would take her property. It must, however, be remembered that this rule was liable to be modified by the custom of women marrying women (see p. 83).

At Qkpanam the eldest son gets his mother's property and has to give his consent to any donations by his mother, otherwise they would be inoperative, even though the property had been acquired by trading. The eldest daughter, however, gets her mother's ikẹṅga, cloth, cooking pots, fowls, baskets, and grinding stones. A mother may give beads to her daughter during life, but they are only a loan unless the umunna are called as witnesses. Even then it appears that after the death of the mother a doctor may order the beads to be restored to the eldest son. In the absence of gifts by the mother, beads, anklets, and the like go to the eldest son. The house, which in the Awka district is sometimes subject to a different rule from the rest of the property, is at Qkpanam broken down at the death of its occupant.

At Isele Asaba a woman's son is her heir. In the absence of a son, the daughter can take certain kinds of property, probably only household goods; a cow and other valuable articles would go to the husband.

At Onitsha Olona the son takes all his mother's property, save household goods, and if the female children were small even these would pass from them.

At Ala valuable property goes to the son, cooking pots and old cloth to the daughter, and the house is broken down. In the absence of children the husband is the heir. If she has a daughter and no sons a woman can divert the property from her brother, who would be her natural heir in the absence of a husband, sons or stepsons, to her daughter. The brother would have to be called, but could not hinder the gift.

At Ibuzǫ, though the eldest daughter takes nothing by right, the cooking pots may go to her, and a woman may purchase in her lifetime ivory and coral and present them to her daughter after informing her husband. If she has no sons and no husband the husband's brother is the next heir if he buries her.

At Oboluku the eldest son gets his mother's property and may give portions to his brothers. The daughters get pots and the like. If there are daughters and no sons, the eldest daughter takes charge of the property and gives some to her sisters. Failing daughters the ǫkpala of her umunna takes all. In accordance with the general rule he takes the property of all whom he buries, whether man or woman. If, however, a woman dies in debt the obi buries her and the debt is not paid.

At Onitsha Ubwo, in the absence of sons, the daughter may inherit all. In a case that came under my notice the eldest of a family of four daughters took all her mother's property, valuable and otherwise. If, however, she married and died without a child her husband would have to return all that she brought to his house. If the other sisters died without a husband the eldest half-brother would get the property. A woman can make gifts on her deathbed, but the heir must be present. She cannot give valuable beads, but may deal with cows as she likes.

At Ubulubu a woman's heir was her eldest son, next to him came her husband, then her husband's eldest son, and finally her brother or ǫkpalębo.

It must, of course, be noted that the eldest son in all cases means the eldest son by the husband with whom she is living, for if a woman leaves her husband she leaves her property behind, as has been seen in the section on woman's property. Anything that she gains or obtains in the house of her new husband is therefore the property of her children by him.

Where a woman has no son, her daughter, though she is not reckoned as idębwe, may refuse to go to her husband,

and have a friend. In this case the daughter may inherit on behalf of her son, otherwise the heir gets all and the daughter does not even get the cooking pots.

At Ezi if a woman goes to her people her own son will bury her and take all her property. If there were no son her brother would inherit. Her daughter can get such property as goats and ačanu beads. If an idẹbwe dies without a son her ọkpala buries her and takes the property, but if she has either a whole or half brother he would be the heir in preference to the ọkpala.

At Idumuje Uboko a husband succeeds to the valuables of a wife in the absence of a son.

At Ukunzu a daughter can get the cooking pots of her mother only if she has not gone to her husband. If there were no qualified daughter, a son would take all; failing a son, her eldest step-son, who also gets the price of all the sisters.

At O ọ pa the rule with regard to the inheritance of woman's property seems to be slightly different. According to the statement made to me, which was, however, not verified, a woman's heirs are firstly her eldest son, secondly her eldest daughter, thirdly her husband, or, if she is living alone, her brother. She may make gifts only to her own children.

LAND.—In the Asaba district, as elsewhere, there is a clear distinction between house land and farm land. House land is invariably private property, but farm land is only rarely so. Under ordinary circumstances, each quarter or each idumu lays claim to the farm land in a certain direction, and the whole town strenuously resists any encroachment upon their farm land, even though it may be claimed by a particular quarter.

In Asaba, the eldest son inherits the house, and his brothers build near him when they are old enough to get houses of their own. It is clearly in this way that the various sub-divisions have arisen. In small towns the ẹbo or quarter is no larger than the idumu or even the umunna of large towns like Asaba or Ibuzọ.

Where two quarters or two persons claim the same area of bush, which is commonly marked beforehand with a knot of grass, or by putting down stones, the ordinary procedure is for the claimant to swear alose. This does not prevent the actual occupant from planting, but merely establishes the ownership of the land. In the case of a quarrel the boundary may be marked by alose, otherwise various trees, a hillock, stones, etc., may mark the division.

If there is trouble between the eldest son and his brothers, they can go to their mother's quarter and reside, but if they wish to take a title, they are compelled to return to their own quarter. If a native of the town has a serious quarrel with a large portion of the community, for example, his umunna or the whole of his idumu, he is sometimes boycotted. This may happen if he is fined and has refused to pay his fine. Under these circumstances, if the boycotted man comes to a meeting, the meeting would break up. If he enters a house, the persons in it leave the house. Before a man who is thus nsopo (outlawed) can be restored, he has to pay the fine and beg the community to take him back.

At Isele Asaba, excommunication takes place before the aniuku and ębwo tree. Ago's ibudu and ǫsisi are brought and struck upon the ground and a goat is offered. The price for restoring a man to his former position is twenty bags.

At Ala, the obwęlani (p. 44) call a meeting to decide when a man shall be boycotted. When this is done he has no public dealing with the ǫkpala of his umunna; he can, however, deal with ordinary people and, in urgent matters such as the payment of bride price, can communicate secretly with the ǫkpala.

If a man builds a house anywhere but in the immediate neighbourhood of his family house, he pays no money but takes palm wine to ask permission.

In a land which has been newly occupied, it is possible in many cases for a man to build where he pleases. This is the case at Idumuje Uboko and Ani Ǫfo (provided it is within the ębo), where the rule prevailed that even a member of the

PLATE **XIV.**

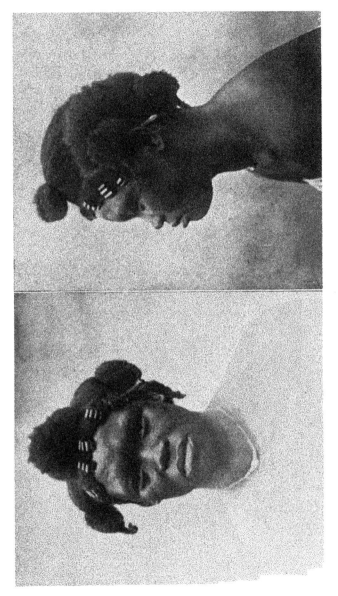

WOMAN OF ISELE ASABA WITH ǪDO ABODA HAIR.

town could be expelled for quarrelling, and sent back to Idumuje Uṇọ, the parent town.

At Onitsha Ubwo, the head of each ẹbo is held to own the land under the obi, and he can give leave to build either to a member of another ẹbo or to a stranger.

At Ukunzu, where there is abundance of land, a man can build where he pleases, but the site of an ancestor's house would be regarded as private property.

At Obọmpa the rule is the same, and it is laid down that the first-born son has a claim upon the site of his father's house even if he has built his own house elsewhere. The conditions are somewhat different where it is a question of permitting a stranger to build.

At Ibuzọ, land is granted for no specified time and the grant cannot be revoked as long as the stranger and his family behave themselves. If he is troublesome, he is told to leave the town, and is apparently permitted to carry off the roof of the house if he wishes.

At g ashi, a stranger gets leave from his host, but he can be expelled by a meeting of the ẹbo.

At Obuluku, a stranger gets permission to build from the head of the family near whom he wishes to settle. If he does not get on with them well, he can be expelled, and in that case he cannot take away the roof. No one will, however, occupy his house. If he leaves his house he can apparently put a price upon it in case he does not return. If he decides to sell it he receives money. If another stranger becomes the owner under these circumstances, and is expelled as an undesirable, he is permitted to remove the roof when he goes, on the ground that he has paid for it.

At Idumuje Uboko, if a stranger builds a house he can hand it over to anyone he likes when he goes. If he does not do so, it must be allowed to fall into ruin. A quarrelsome stranger can be expelled and another man put in charge of his house, and he virtually becomes the owner. The stranger can dig his yams but not remove the roof; his trees he would leave in charge.

At Ani Ọfo, a stranger builds where he likes, and the idumu in which he resides temporarily will give him assistance. A quarrelsome stranger can be turned out, and in this case the house either falls into disrepair or is taken possession of by anyone who wants the house. The owner's leave is not necessary for this, as he can neither sell nor pawn the house nor yet remove the roof.

At Idumuje Ụnọ, a stranger is taken by the head of the ebo to the obi, who gives him permission to build. He is compelled to build near the house of the ọkpalẹbo, probably with the idea of enabling the ọkpalẹbo to keep a watchful eye upon him. A quarrelsome stranger can be expelled by the obi at will. He cannot sell his house, but may hand it over to another man, whether stranger or otherwise.

At Onitsha Ubwo, a stranger can be expelled, and in this case he cannot hand over his house to anyone, but if he is leaving without palaver, he can give it to a friend. · He is not allowed to sell it, nor yet to take the roof away.

A quarrelsome stranger can be expelled at Ukunzu, and he can neither sell his house nor remove the roof.

At O ọ pa, a stranger cannot sell his house, and the reason given to me was that he had not bought the land on which it stood. The ọkpalẹbo gives leave to a stranger to build, and the young men of the ẹbo will give him assistance. If a stranger turns out to be quarrelsome, a meeting is called and he can be expelled. In this case the house falls in and a man can take away the materials if he likes; I was told that an Ubwodu man, who came seven years before, had left the year before I was in the town. He took some of the good wood with him, but apparently was not allowed to remove the roof. He might also have assigned the materials to the ọkpalumunna or have assigned the house as a whole to the ọkpala to grant to anyone he liked.

At Ubulubu, where the bush, ọnumbana, round a man's house is reckoned as his property, a stranger asks his host for land, and if he is to be expelled, his host is informed. A stranger refuses to go occasionally, and is then compelled to pay a fine and take an oath before ani. The roof cannot be removed, as the house is on the land of the Ubulubu people, nor yet can a stranger sell it. His former host takes it as his own.

At Ezi, if a stranger comes, the obi, who is held to own all the land, gives him permission to build. If he is troublesome, the obi orders him out on the recommendation of the head of the ẹbo. The house goes to the ọkpalẹbo and no payment is due, for it is held that the wood does not belong to the builder of the house. A stranger can take the yams if they are nearly ripe, or can revisit the town to dig them up, but, generally speaking, the trees and the farm of the stranger belong to the head of the ẹbo. If a man leaves without palaver, he can sell his trees to the head of the quarter, but cannot dispose of either the house or the roof; he can at most hand it over to a friend. The children, however, of the original settler are held to be natives of the town and cannot be driven away.

Farm Land.—At Ibuzọ farm land is private property and is inherited from father to son, at any rate in some of the quarters. It can be sold after giving information to the ọkpalumunna, but, before this is done, all the umunna must be summoned to give assistance. If no buyer is found among them the seller has complete freedom to sell. He would, however, only sell from one akwu (see p. 175) and when it came to the turn of this to be cleared for farms he would beg other people for a share. The explanation of this appropriation of farm land in Ibuzọ is probably to be found in the fact that it is an extremely large town (40,000 inhabitants, according to the last census), wedged in between Asaba and Qkpanam. Very little land, comparatively speaking, is therefore available. This was the only instance of individual ownership of farm land which I found in the Asaba district. Ordinarily, as has been stated above, each quarter owns the land to which its farm road leads. In Asaba anyone may plant on the land of any quarter but before he does this he must get permission, which will only be given if he is known to be a good husbandman. In addition to individuals there seem to be certain small towns settled on Asaba land ; they hold their farm land on the same indefinite title ; they are not regarded as owners, but on the other hand they can hardly be expelled.

· At Oboluku each ẹbo owns the farm land along its mbana or farm road. Each idumu goes out and clears for itself, but if there is not sufficient land some of the men may go elsewhere.

At Idumuje Ụnọ, in the same way, each ẹbo has its own farm road and anyone may go and make his farm where he likes, provided it is not already appropriated by someone else. The idumu may unite to deal with the big bush, but men are free to group themselves as they like.

At Ubulubu each ẹbo has its own " way to farm " although there appears to be an abundance of land and the place was only settled some 50 years ago. A payment of twenty-five yams is exacted for permission to plant on the land of another ẹbo. The term is fixed and a goat is sacrificed to the ani. This difference in custom is doubtless due to the fact that one of the quarters is of Yoruba stock, and, as has been stated elsewhere, their proper language is Yoruba to this day. Ezi people say that Ubulubu lives on their land and gave a woman as a wife to purchase the ground on which they build. No tribute has ever been asked but some 15 years ago Ubulubu encroached on the Ezi farm land, with the result that the Obwobi quarter of Ezi have only sufficient land for four annual farms, whereas other quarters return after seven years. Ubulubu in their turn stand upon their rights ; if Obọmpa crosses their boundary they cut ọmu and plant in the ground where the Ohọmpa people are clearing the bush. This will probably cause them to stop, otherwise Ezi people gather iyi for the Obọmpa people to swear upon. The Obọmpa people have oil palms on the land which the Ubulubu people are not allowed to touch; similarly the Ubulubu people have ọma leaves for making mats and roofing houses which O ọ pa cannot touch.

Apparently trespass by domestic animals causes little

PLATE XV.

WALL PAINTINGS: LEOPARD PURSUING BUSH-BUCK.

trouble, for the farms are usually at a considerable distance from the town. At Oboluku they are some 3 miles away on one road; and when I enquired why they did not make Ubweni, the small farm commonly found near the house, they replied they did not want to clear the bush because they liked to have the squirrels about.

Although farm land may not be sold it must be remembered that a farm with growing crops is private property and can be disposed of. Details will be found under the heading of farm.

TREES.—In Asaba a distinction is drawn between trees on private property, trees on cultivated farms and trees in the bush. Individuals who own trees such as oil palms, kokonut, bread fruit, raphia, iroko, kola or plum (ube), can sell them if necessary to anyone. A tree in the farm is the property of the farmer so long as the farm is actually in cultivation. The head of the quarter is regarded as the owner of all trees in the bush, but if he sells them he must inform the quarter or idumu, and after deducting his own share, divide the remainder obtained from the sale. It sometimes happens that if the head of the quarter dies and his successor is a poor man, he pawns the abo (plantation of palm trees, etc.) to a richer man. This he can do, apparently, without notifying the quarter, and redeem the plantation later. If, however, he finds himself unable to do this, a subsequent sale is a matter of concern to the whole of the quarter and they must be invited, so that they may subscribe if they wish to retain the land.

The law as to the ownership of fruits differs from the ordinary law and is not uniform for all fruits. If a kokonut falls the finder can take it; if he picks up okwa it is not theft, but the owner can call upon him to return it. Fallen kola can be taken. As regards pawning, the pawnee has free access whether the land be his own or not, and if the tree dies he takes the wood.

At Qkpanam the ordinary rule is that trees near a man's house are his property, and the same rule prevails with regard

to trees in or near the border of a farm with certain exceptions. Trees in the bush not planted by anyone are the
common property of the ẹbo. I was told, however, that a
plantation of kola, okwa and similar trees belonged to the
owner of the land, even if he did not plant them himself, but
this was a point on which I failed to get any clear information. On the other hand I was told that if a man made a
farm, ubwẹni, enclosing a plantation, the owner of the
plantation had access to his trees at any time. It is
probable, therefore, that the planter is the owner of the
trees. If a kola tree is burned in a farm another one may
assigned in its place or the owner may receive a slave in
compensation. As regards ordinary trees fire wood may be
cut anywhere except near the border of a farm, which can
only be utilised if permission has been given.

Palm trees near a man's house are his property, but if he
assigns the plot to another man, the ownership of the tree
does not pass even if the house of the new owner is nearer
to the tree. A palm tree near a farm, say 4 or 6 yards
from the edge of the farm, is not regarded as the property of
the farmer. An ojuku tree is not used, save that the fibre
is taken to make the aziza on the hat of an ẹze. Other
people are permitted to take the nuts. They do not cut it
down, but there is no penalty if one is felled by mistake. If
a new farm is made for another year beyond a man's farm,
the head of the quarter will ask the owner of the old farm
whether he wants the portion immediately beyond, known as
isi ani.

An iroko tree on a man's house land is his own property
and he would not even give permission to another man to fell
it. If a tree has been felled in the farm before the land has
been cleared and lies on two persons' farms, they share it and
the head of the quarter has nothing to do with it. On the
road to farm or in an unmade farm the decision as to whether
it may be felled rests with the ẹke ebo who receives one or
more doors from the wood after it is felled. If a man burns
an iroko tree in the farm till it falls, he calls a carpenter

and shares with him; but if in thus felling the tree he spoils a man's yams, two doors are paid in compensation. A kola tree in the bush is the common property of the ẹbo, but the finder may transplant a small kola tree.

If a kokonut is too near a house that is being built, the owner, if he belongs to the same umunna, would give permission to the builder to fell the tree. If they were only in the same idumu, however, the builder would be called upon to give a substitute or might give two kola trees. Any trees can be sold or pawned. A woman can own trees, but they seldom plant them and the husband is probably regarded as the real owner. A son cannot take the fruits from his father's tree without permission. They believe that he would die if he attempted to do so. -

At Isele Asaba oil palms near a house are private property, but those on the street are common property. Trees in or near a farm are the property of the farmer; other trees such as ube, bread fruit, kola, kokonut, a creeper named okba and ẹbwo, which is used for fences, are private property either in the street or on house land.

At Onitsha Olona the head of the ẹbo owns all trees in the street, oil palms excepted. Kola, kokonut, ube, etc., all belong to him if they are not planted by anyone and he can give them to anyone. An oil palm is common property unless it is close to a house. If a man leaves his house his next neighbour claims the tree.

At Ala the ọkpalẹbo claims the trees known as ife aku, that is, all trees planted by the original founder of the quarter and all seedlings from them. He is therefore held to be the owner of all trees, save such as are on house land or on actually cultivated farms, whether they are in the town or in the bush. Anyone, however, is entitled to cut palm nuts or take palm wine unless he is forbidden by the ọkpalẹbo. The ọkpalẹbo can take all the produce but cannot sell the trees. Apparently his ownership of trees in the town is more of a reality than in the case of trees outside the town. An individual owns all trees that he plants, including oil palm trees; but anyone, I was told, can claim a kokonut tree which is derelict, though this would appear to conflict with the rights of the ǫkpalębo. Kola also can be claimed by the finder if he clears the space round it.

In the case of iroko a doctor must first of all be called to divine what is to be done. He may, for example, order an egg to be broken on the tree as a sacrifice or a chicken to be offered. Besides this, if a man asks permission to cut down an iroko, the ǫkpalębo calls a meeting of the elders, whose consent is necessary before the tree can be felled, unless the ǫkpalębo himself wishes to do it. Consent is always necessary for the sale of the tree, and the money is shared by the ikei ębo, that is to say, by the ǫkpalębo and the three or four that come next to him. They probably include in practice the actual oldest man in each umunna, and any olinzęle, such as Odogu, the ęz' ikolǫbia, and the okaibwa; the latter, however, gets no share. I was told that in recent years two iroko trees had been cut down, and that only 5s. had been received in all. They were of opinion that, inasmuch as a native carpenter was prepared to pay £5 for a tree, the royalty payable to the quarter should be nearer the actual value of the tree. If £5 were paid the shares would be approximately as follows: 25s. to the ǫkpalębo, 15s. to the man second to him, and 30s. for the umunna of each idumu.

At Ibuzǫ oil palms and other trees are private property in the town; the kokonut tree in particular is owned by the man who planted it, whether it is on his own land or not. Trees in the farm may be cut for firewood, but iroko only by permission of the owner of the farm; he may make arrangements to share with the sawyer or sell it for £5. The ǫkpalumunna keeps some of the money from the sale of his own iroko, hands some to the rest of the umunna, and gives a share to the ǫkpalębo. An ordinary man, however, gives a share to the ǫkpalumunna and keeps the remainder himself. This difference is due to the fact that, firstly, certain kinds of tribute are due from the ǫkpalumunna to the ǫkpalębo, and, secondly, that the ǫkpalumunna is the trustee to the umunna, and property is vested in him as their representative.

At g ashi the obi is held to be the owner of all the land, but this does not materially alter the law with regard to the ownership of trees. A palm tree in the farm, for example, belongs to the farmer so long as he is cultivating the plot. Plantations of banana in a farm remain private property for three years, and the same is true of other trees on the road to farm.

Anyone who wishes to cut an iroko tree must apply to the obi through his head chief, and the payment is said to be £7, half of which goes to the ikei ani, but I failed to discover the exact distribution, for the same informant went on to say that the obi got one share with his ębo, Iyase got one share with the three obwe known collectively as Osani, and Onirhe and Odafe got one share, which was also partitioned with others of their ębo. A kola tree, if it is on the land of a man's own ębo, can be claimed by him if he cleans the bush round it. Anyone may take up fallen kola or kokonut, but okwa may not be picked up by a man save of the same umunna.

At Oboluku oil palms close to a house are owned with the house. The idumu are owners of oil palms in the town. Anyone can cut in the bush, and the trees growing in a farm are vested in the owner of the farm. Okwa, kola, kokonut and other trees are owned by the planter, even though another house is subsequently built nearer to them. An iroko is owned by the ębo, and anyone who wishes to cut it applies to the head of the ębo, who gets a share of the objects made from it. No one else in the ębo is entitled to a share. Trees can be pawned or sold, but kola or kokonut, the value of which is 5s., only by a man who has no one to assist him. Plantain or banana trees are not pawned or sold.

At Onitsha Ubwo the oil palm close to a house or in a

cultivated farm is owned, others are common property if they have not been planted. Other trees are owned by the planter, save that plantain, banana, and m mi mi are common property in the bush. Kokonut and kola can be pawned or sold if a man is in great need, the value being for pawning 1s. 3d. or selling 2s. 6d. An iroko in the compound of a man's house is his property, in the bush it is owned by the ẹbo, that is to say, by the head of the ẹbo that goes that way to farm.

At Idumuje kokonut and oil palm in a man's yard are his private property. A farmer owns them as long as he cultivates the farm. A planted kokonut, plantain, or banana are permanent property, and a man can return to the old farm for produce, which no one else can lawfully cut; he would probably try to remove the trees. The fruit from derelict property can be cut unless it is on the road to farm. As regards oil palms, though they are owned by the man near whose house they stand, anyone is at liberty to use them for palm wine. In the street they are common property. Anyone can take abwọno in the middle of another man's farm.

A plum tree planted in the bush is private property; one not planted cannot be claimed. If a man has planted a plum tree he cleans the bush and makes a heap of brush-wood round it, but anyone may pick up the fruit without being liable to a charge of theft. Anyone may clear a space round a chance sapling, but only with the idea of enabling the tree to grow well. He has no special claim upon the fruit. If a man finds a kola tree in the bush he has to make a clearance round it every year, though omission to do so would not necessarily invalidate his claim. He would ordinarily put rope round it and tie iyi to it. If, in the course of burning the bush, a kola tree is destroyed, no claim for compensation can be made. An iroko is owned by the obi, and he receives any money that is paid for it. It may be noted with regard to iroko that here, as elsewhere, anyone that makes ọkpala title plants an iroko tree, which is cut down at his death to make a coffin, regardless of the forestry regulations. O k w a, o p i p i (bitter kola) and other trees are owned by the planter near his house, but are common in the bush.

At Ani Qfo, a very recent settlement, the rules with regard to trees are different. I r o k o in the bush can be felled by anyone, though now the chief is notified, and a payment is made both to the chief and to native court funds. Bananas and plantain are planted when they fire the farm, and bear fruit after the seed yams are dug. After this anyone can take the fruit, even though they are on the road to farm or to water; the fruit once cut off is private property; neither banana nor plantain trees are sold. An a b w ǫ n o tree is common property unless it is close to a house, and even then the seed may be picked up. Kola, kokonut, u b e and other trees may be sold by a man who is leaving the town.

At Ukunzu no one plants oil palms, but those which grow in the compound or cultivated farms are the property of the owner. A number of trees, including u b e, a b w ǫ n o, kola, kokonut and others are planted and owned. Fallen o k b a can be picked up, and the same is true of kokonut. O k w a cannot be picked up. O k w a and kola found in the bush can be claimed by the man who makes a clearing, but anyone in the ǫ b o can help himself at pleasure. Kola, kokonut, and o k w a can be sold, the price being about 5s., and the same three trees, and u b e in addition, may be pawned. If the kokonut tree dies, the debt is extinguished and the broker takes the wood. Anyone can throw wood at the u b e tree and knock the fruit down, and it cannot be claimed. Generally speaking, taking fruits is not regarded as stealing where both parties are of the same ǫ b o.

At O ǫ pa anyone can fell the i r o k o in the bush; a b w ǫ n o and o d a l a are common property. A banana tree is owned in the farm, and as long as the bush is cleared round it. When a new farm is made there the farmer must be notified. If a kola tree is found in the bush, a man may clear the ground round it and claim it if it is too small to bear fruit, otherwise it is common property. Kola on the ground, even in a man's compound, may be picked up. The okwa tree, on the other hand, is not climbed to obtain fruit, and fallen fruit is taken to the owner, or word is brought to him. The owner of an ube tree may use hard words to those who throw at it to get the plums, but cannot demand them back. Kola, kokonut, and okwa may be pawned, the two former for about 5s. and the latter for about 4d.

At Ubulubu they have the following trees: (1) Abwǫno, (2) Kokonut, (3) Kola, (4) Lime, (5) Oil palm, (6) Okba, (7) Okwa, (8) Orange, (9) Ube, (10) Ugili. In the bush these are common property, but, if they have not begun to bear, a man may clear the ground round them and claim them. Kola found in the farm may be saved from fire and claimed. Kola, kokonut, and okwa may be sold or pawned, but, if more than the recognised sum, namely, 5s., were accepted on the pawn, it would be equivalent to sale. An ube tree may be sold only when a man is removing. Anyone can throw at an ube tree, but only the umunna can claim it to obtain the fruits. Ubulubu was settled only some 50 years ago; up to that time the site was dense forest, and all oil palms were originally planted; those on the road to farm, however, are now regarded as common property. Iroko is not regarded as private property.

At Ezi trees in the farm belong to the farmer until the new seed has been put in the ground; after this anyone may pick cotton or use the trees. Most iroko trees are common, but those planted during the ceremony of taking titles belong to a man and his descendants. If a stranger obtains permission from the obi or the head of the ębo, he takes what he wants, and gives three doors to the head of the ębo, who owns the logs left over. I was also told that any man may take a guest to fell iroko without asking permission.

The practice with regard to oil palms is that those on the

land of an ẹbo belong to an ẹbo, but the fruits of those in the bush can be cut, even by a stranger. A young kola can be transplanted and owned unless it is on the farm road, where land is common. The same is true of ugili and abwọno near the house; ube can also be transplanted or or cleared. A banana tree is owned by the planter even in the farm, and anyone else who takes fruit must inform the owner, or else it may be treated as theft. In the case of a man who is taking a title, permission is sometimes given him by the owners of trees to gather at will.

WATER.—Although the ownership of a stream is frequently a matter of conflict between one town and another in the present day, it does not appear that any part of a town lays special claim to a stream which is within the boundaries of the whole town, though as regards fishing rights a claim may be set up.

In addition to streams water is obtained from so-called wells. These are holes usually dug in the centre of the street and often lightly fenced round. Sometimes three or more may be found one after the other, all belonging to the same quarter, with an iyi of some sort to prevent strangers from infringing their rights.

At Onitsha Olona a well is dug by the umunna and vested in the head of the umunna. Anyone may take water from it in the rainy season, but in the dry season the ọkpala, in whom it is vested, puts iyi on it and a stranger must ask leave before drawing water. No one may dig a hole near a man's house. The ogodo (mud hole) at Onitsha Olona belongs to the nze of the ẹbo, but all the ẹbo can work there.

In connection with water rights may be mentioned the law regarding the digging of chalk (kaolin) at Ukunzu. Anyone from the whole town is at liberty to procure the chalk, which is treated as a water product.

TAKING CHARGE.—It is a common practice in the Asaba district for an owner of live stock, large or small, to hand over one or more head to relatives or friends for them to take charge of, and the holder of them is rewarded by gifts of one or more of the young.

At Qkpanam, where a goat is given to a man to look after, he gets the third, fifth, seventh kid, and so on, and, in consideration, pays seven yams a year to the owner and provides palm wine and yams on the occasion of any sacrifice. The mother and kid would be reclaimed if the dues were not paid. If the goat dies the body is sold and the owner takes the money so that a new goat may be bought; it is brought to the owner so that he may put his property mark upon it. If it were stolen the holder pays no compensation even if negligence were proved, but he is responsible if he alleges theft without being able to prove it.

At Isele Asaba a man who receives a cow in charge gives sixty kola, cowries to the value of 6d. and palm wine to the owner, who can call him to work upon his farm. When the fourth calf is born the holder brings 60 yams, 140 kola, a long broom, a small broom, and palm oil. The owner offers kola to the mwǫ and the calf becomes the property of the holder, who receives one out of every four as long as he keeps the cow. In the case of a goat he gives 6d. in cowries to the owner when he receives it, and sends kola, seven yams, and palm wine, for the first kid, the third, and so on, and keeps them. For a dog the dues are the same and the litter is divided equally. In the case of a fowl five yams, twenty cowries, and one pot of palm wine are the dues, and the chickens are divided equally when they are grown.

At Onitsha Olona before a man hands over a cow to a friend to be taken charge of the friend has to be importunate. The umunna of the owner will take the cow and receive ten ngugu from the man who is to have it in charge. Three ngugu are paid to the owner and one and a half to those who actually hold the cow. At dawn the next day the holder comes with his umunna to the owner of the cow and fires a gun. He gives kola to his umunna. From that day the owner and the holder are reckoned as relatives in law (ǫgǫ), and the holder serves as they serve for a wife. He brings wood and yams at intervals, works on the farm at times with others of his ẹbo, and, at the annual sacrifice to the mwǫ, brings five yams, sixty kola, and sixty okba. The holder keeps the owner informed of the condition of the cow and if it dies the meat is shared between owner and holder. A bull calf goes to the owner and if the second is a cow the owner will take it also, but if both are females one will go to the holder, who brings a goat, 300 yams, 2 brooms, 60 mbannu, and 60 kola, and goes to the owner with friends from his ẹbo. After this he gets no further share of the young and will probably hand the cow over to one of his umunna.

In the case of a goat twins would be divided. If the kids are female they go alternately to owner and holder, and the same if they are all males. But if the first two are male and female, both go to the owner and the third to the holder. In the case of a dog five yams only are given, at some time not fixed by custom, and five yams when they share the litter. If the holder of a fowl is a woman she makes soup and brings the chickens to divide. In hunger time she cooks a yam dish known as okbǫ. If the holder is a man he brings five yams and works for the owner.

At Ala the umunna of the owner bring the cow and receive a goat and 5s. The goat is divided between the umunna and the owner and the holder. The visiting umunna is taken round the ẹbo and receives kola and cowries. The holder has to work on the owner's farm and pay tribute at Iwaji. When the first calf is born, ten yams, ten pots of palm wine, and ten kola go to the owner. The second calf goes to the holder, who pays twenty yams, seven pots of palm wine, and 100 kola ; but the remainder of the calves go to the owner, but the holder of a cow keeps it in charge and does service for it till it dies or is sold. In the case of a goat, kids go alternately to owner and holder; when they go the owner kola and palm wine only are payable; where the holder takes them he also takes seven yams.

At Ibuzọ the owner takes the first six calves and the holder takes the seventh. His annual dues are sixty yams, palm wine, tobacco, and fish. The holder only gets one calf, and if the cow dies before he gets it his only compensation is a goat and 5s. In the case of a goat the third kid goes to the holder. If it bears two or three kids at once they are not divided. If the goat dies the body is sent to the owner. The only dues are a basket of corn and a load of yams, but nothing is payable when the holder takes the kid. In the case of a fowl the holder tells the owner when it is laying eggs, and the chickens are shared equally.

At g ashi the holder takes only one calf and pays in return three bags of cowries, many yams, oil and soap. The third kid goes to the holder, who takes yams, kola, palm wine, and five ngugu to the owner, and offers kola to his ikẹṅga. After that every second kid is the holder's.

At Idumuje, on the day that a cow is sent by its owner, the conductors get a calabash of meat which they share with the umunna of the owner. The third calf goes to the holder, who pays sixty yams and one bag on the day he receives it. In the case of a goat, the kids go alternately, and five yams and a calabash of palm wine are payable by the holder when it comes to his turn. A woman makes cloth and brings salt and palm oil.

At Obọmpa a man who wishes to have a cow in charge takes 150 yams, 100 kola, 40 bags of salt, and palm oil to the owner. He pays one bag to the conductors of the cow, most of which goes to the owner. The dues are five yams at Mwarọ and five yams at New Yams. If the second calf is a female it goes to the holder, who gives 100 yams, 60 bags of salt, 15s., and ugili and pepper.

At Ubulubu the method for obtaining a cow is somewhat roundabout. A man who wishes to obtain one will do service to the owner, but, apparently, not ask him directly. The owner then tells a third person that the candidate has been

PLATE XVI.

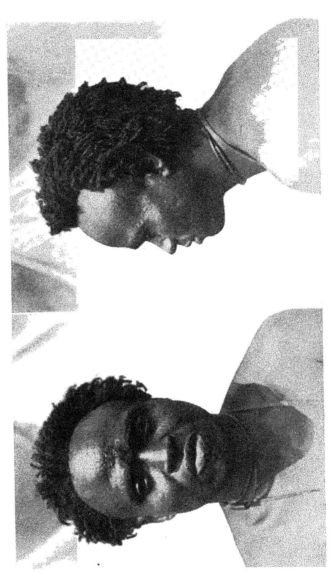

YOUNG MAN OF IBUZǪ.

doing him service, on which it is permissible to beg for the cow. A goat, 100 yams and 20 mbannu are payable on the day he receives the cow, and his umunna say "Omajigǫ koko," "He does well." The holder brings annually five yams and a calabash of palm wine to offer to the ikǫṅga, in order that the cow may produce calves. The sixth goes to the holder, the cow is transferred back to the owner, and the service is at an end.

DEBT.—The normal practice of Southern Nigerian tribes appears to be for a creditor to seize the property, in some cases also persons, if the debt is of sufficient amount, belonging to the debtor, or forming one of his social unit, that is to say, in most cases the umunna. It must be borne in mind that among primitive peoples and peoples among whom law is in a comparatively undeveloped condition, the responsibility for acts of omission and commission does not stop with the person actually implicated according to our ideas, but extends to his blood relatives and to those of more remote kin whom we should at most designate connections if we recognised any bond of relationship. Thus, it will be seen in the section on Murder that a man's brother may be put to death if the murderer himself cannot be brought to justice; and it was shown in the report on the Awka Ibo that, in addition to the murderer and his immediate relatives, a wide circle might suffer loss of property through his wrongdoing.

This method of seizure is found also in the Asaba district with the same or even greater extension of responsibility of the kin. The creditor can seize any object equal in value to the debt, not only from the umunna of his debtor, but in the idumu or in the ǫbo. When it is remembered that, at the present day, the Asaba ǫbo includes on an average 4,000 persons, it will be seen that the creditor has wide scope. After seizing the property the creditor has to call the debtor, and grace of one or even two months may be accorded the latter, during which time the property remains in the custody of the creditor. If the debt is not satisfied within a reasonable time the idumu or ǫbo of the debtor has to be notified,

M

though, of course, the fact of the seizure would be known to them long before; and if they do not intervene the property may be sold in satisfaction of the debt. It would, however, usually happen that the immediate kin of the debtor would raise a subscription and redeem the pawn, though in the case of a confirmed wastrel they would probably let matters take their course.

At Asaba itself neither trees nor yams could be seized, whether the latter were yet in the farm or already stored. At Ibuzọ, on the other hand, yams could be seized for debts of certain kinds, but in the case actually cited to me the seizure was more in the way of an enforcement of contract than for the settlement of a debt. I was told that if A sold seed yams to B, and in spite of that planted them on his own farm, B could go to the farm and take the yams.

Another method of dealing with debt at Ibuzọ was for the creditor to go three times to the debtor, and on the last occasion to take with him four men of his own umunna. They seized as many goats in the streets as would cover the debt, apparently only in the umunna of the debtor. The owner of a seized goat would look for it with a bell, and the man who seized it would declare the cause. It appears that if goats are seized under these circumstances and held or sold in satisfaction of the debt, the original debtor is free of his debt, for one of the umunna would not claim from another. The saying on this point is "Ụgwọ ṅwanna nana n'antoto asia," "the debt of a kinsman goes by proverb"; the meaning being that one of the umunna does not pay another. Where the debtor is in another town, seizure apparently is the only means of compelling payment.

There was, however, another method of proceeding in case of debt, and this was to employ the services of one or more titled men, that is to say, ẹze at Asaba, or dibia, or one of the dignitaries. At Asaba a creditor could recover his debt as follows: He called upon the ẹze and put a leaf in the aperture of his ivory horn, telling him that a certain person owed him money. Thereupon the ǫze went to the debtor's house after 6 p.m. For reasons to be explained later, the debtor was desirous of preventing the ǫze from sleeping in his house. He asked his idumu to come out and beg the ǫze to return, at the same time promising to satisfy his creditor. If the ǫze left, he received a goat to sacrifice to his mwǫ. If, on the other hand, the debtor did not beg the ǫze, then all the ǫze of the idumu from which the original ǫze came, would leave their houses and sit down in the house of the debtor. In this case the debtor would probably make an effort to pay his debt and get the ǫze to leave his house before dawn. If dawn came, a goat had to be paid or ndi ǫze would at once seize the property of the debtor, and inform his idumu that all his property was vested in them (the ǫze). Thereupon the friends of the debtor would come to beg for mercy, and the debtor himself would provide a chicken, a cock, a goat, and 7s., which would be handed to the ǫze. If, in addition, the debtor gave satisfactory assurances the property would be released. If, however, they were not satisfied the ǫze would take ǫmu (a young palm leaf) and tie it round the farm of the debtor. This would stop the debtor from using his farm, but at the same time the creditor was prevented from using it. The result was that if the debt was not paid the farm was ruined.

At Isele Asaba the creditor complained to Ago, who sent one of his slaves, known as Isokute, to sleep in the house of the debtor. If possible the debtor satisfied his creditor as soon as Isokute arrived. If, however, Isokute slept in the house of the debtor, the latter had to provide a chicken and a cock to purify Isokute, who also changed his cloth and threw the old one away, the debtor being responsible for providing a new one. One goat was also paid to Isokute. Then the Ikei ani (p. 152) met, and Isokute killed a goat and the meat was divided. The creditor was apparently compelled to pawn himself to procure the money, and, failing this, to go to Ago, head chief, who satisfied the debt.

At Obǫmpa, the creditor went to the Otu Dibia, who would

force the debtor to pay, or, in case of default, would report to the Ouotu. The procedure was for the doctors to go to the debtor's house, each carrying his ǫfǫ, for it was a rule that a doctor might not sleep with ǫfǫ in a man's house. If they did so, a hen had to be found to be offered to the ǫfǫ of each man, and a cock for his orhai. In place of sleeping in a man's house, however, the doctors might, if his assurances were satisfactory, fix a term for the payment of the money. If, on the other hand, the Onotu were called in, they might likewise send their ǫfǫ to the debtor's house, and before it could be taken away, the debt had to be paid and a cock sent for sacrifice to ǫfǫ.

At Ubulubu the head of the doctors sent ǫfǫ to the debtor's house. On the following day all the doctors went with him and the debtor was compelled to pay the debt, and a fine of some 15s. and a cock, into the hands of the head of the doctors, who handed the amount of the debt to the creditor.

This comparatively legal method of securing payment of a debt was due, in part, to a more organised condition in the Asaba district, in part to the fact that any man who seized property belonging to a doctor exposed himself to penalties. It was, therefore, dangerous to sally forth into the streets and seize property at random.

It was possible, as in other parts, for a creditor to assign the debt to one of his own creditors, but this could not be done without the consent of the debtor, and the assignment had to be made in the presence of a witness. It is, of course, a maxim of native law that a debt is not extinguished by lapse of time. So far from their recognising a statute of limitations, a debt may be recognised even after the lapse of three or four generations.

The normal procedure at Asaba was for a man to call his creditors (and likewise his debtors) and make a declaration in the presence of his heirs. If any unnamed creditor presented himself after the death of the debtor, he would be called upon to swear upon an alose, or the money to satisfy

PLATE XVII.

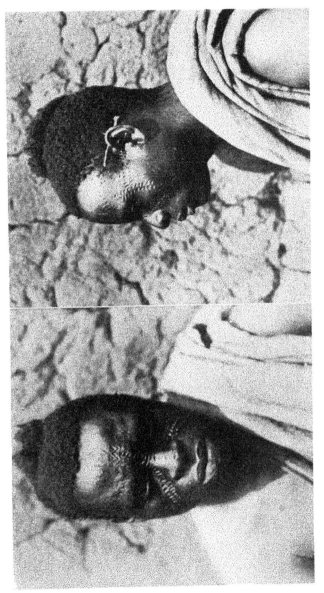

MAN OF OBOLUKU.

the debt would be put upon an alose and the creditor invited to take it, which he would not venture to do if the debt were a fictitious one, or the amount inaccurately stated.

At Ibuzọ the method of proving such a debt was as follows: after fixing a day, various alose were collected and a suitable victim sacrificed to each; a chalk circle was drawn and the alose put inside; the debtor had to stand within the circle, certain words were recited, and the debtor, who would, of course, be an heir of the original debtor, declared that he was ignorant of the existence of the debt. If money were paid to the creditor and he fell sick, this would be put down to the vengeance of the alose; the money was repaid, the same victims purchased for each alose and sacrificed to the alose by their owners. At the same time the alose were begged to set free the man whom they had afflicted with sickness and not to kill him.

Where a debtor died, leaving more debts than the value of his estate, the heir could not divest himself of the responsibility by refusing the estate. Under ordinary circumstances the man who performed the burial ceremonies for a dead man made himself responsible for his debts even if he had no property. In some cases, however, if not all, the nearest male relative could not refuse to accord the rites of burial. A debtor whose umunna was not known, that is to say, either a stranger or a last survivor of his umunna, was buried at Onitsha Olona by the ọkpala of the idumu, who became responsible for the debt.

At Oboluku a dead debtor who had no sons would be buried by the Obi, to whom the debtor would sometimes go in his lifetime to explain the situation, for here his people could refuse to bury him. If this explanation had not been made in advance, the head of the umunna went to the Obi and handed over the property of the deceased, and the creditor lost his money, though, no doubt, this would only happen where the debts exceeded the assets.

At Isele Asaba if a debtor pawned himself and died before his creditor was satisfied the man who buried him took over the debt. If the burial rites were undertaken by his brother and he also had pawned himself, an arrangement would be made by which the debt stood over, or the son of the original debtor could be pawned in his place. I was informed that if the brother paid the debt of a dead man he was compelled to hand over his property entire to a son who was a minor at the time of his father's death, but this appears to be so exceptional that I doubt if the information is accurate.

Loans.—In order to raise money three methods might be adopted. Firstly, money might be lent with or without interest, but without security. In loaning (zinye) without interest no term would, apparently, be fixed for the repayment of the money in some towns. In others the term would be fixed by agreement, perhaps three months, which might, however, be extended. Loans with interest, contrary to the custom on the other side, appear to have been rare. If interest were demanded, in spite of no arrangement having been made, the borrower would put the interest on an alose exactly as would be done in the case of an unproved debt, At Ibuzọ loans with interest were unknown; the loan was handed over before witnesses brought by the two parties, and apparently no term was fixed for repayment.

Pawning.—The normal method, however, of raising money was to pawn a person or pledge property. The pawn was virtually in the position of a slave, that is to say, under ordinary circumstances the produce of his work was the property of the broker, except in so far as the work was done on his free days. The broker, on the other hand, was responsible for providing him, and in some cases also his family, with food. The situation of a pawn was by no means unpleasant; he was in many cases better off in all probability than he would be in his own family, and was sometimes adopted into the family of the broker if he showed himself to be a useful member of society. The fact that a man would sometimes pawn himself, not in satisfaction of a debt or to avoid worse consequences, but in order to procure a wife, is

PLATE XVIII.

WOMAN OF ISELE ASABA.

sufficient evidence that the life of a pawn was not regarded as a hard one.

At Asaba the custom appears to have been to pawn a child of either sex, not to the creditor himself, but to one of the ẹze. If the pawn died, he was buried by his father, and another child had to be given in security or the debt paid. If a girl were pawned the father would always be consulted and decide as to which suitor would be accepted, and the bride price of the pawn or a portion of it was handed over in satisfaction of the debt.

At Isele Asaba a girl might be given to a man as a wife in satisfaction of a debt. At Onitsha Olona a woman could pawn her daughter but only to another woman. A big girl who would soon go to her husband could not be pawned. At Ibuzọ a girl could be pawned to a relative, otherwise it was reckoned as marriage. At g ashi on the other hand a girl would be pawned to anyone, and the broker was allowed to find a suitor for the girl, though the father had to be consulted as usual. At Oboluku girls were pawned to women only, and an arrangement was made at once as to whether the girl should marry the broker's son. At Idumuje U'boko girls were accounted more valuable as pawns than boys because they could work at night at making thread. The suitor could, however, redeem a marriageable girl, handing the money to her father as payment for the creditor. At Ukunzu girls were pawned and also at Obọmpa, where the suitor would usually redeem her. In the latter place the broker might marry the pawn, or, if she were too closely related, the father might assign a friend to her, in which case the children would, according to the general rule, belong to the father. The same rule prevailed at Ezi save that a girl would only be pawned to women. At Ọkpanam and Ala, on the other hand, only male children could be pawned.

At Isele Asaba a man could pledge himself or his son, but apparently could not pledge both himself and his son. Under normal conditions an adult would have one free day on which he would earn money and would also utilise for his own work, the time before the arrival of his master. If a man pledged himself, his wife went home to her mother and explained the situation, but she would follow her husband if possible, and in that case the broker would provide food for the whole family. If a man did not work well it could be recorded against him; a knot was tied in a cord and after a certain number had been tied, the kinsman of the pawn would hear of the matter. This, however, was of comparatively rare occurrence, as the pawn took an oath to serve well. If a pawn vacated his house, one of the idumu could take charge of it and hand it back when the pawn was free. The creditor would work the farm for nothing and set off the money received by the sale of yams against the debt. The broker would provide seed yams for the debtor to plant in his (the broker's) farm. It might also happen that instead of receiving a free day the pawn would get money, that is wages, from the broker. Where the pawn was young, the broker might help him to take a title, and this would place him in the position of a kinsman, though it did not entitle him to inherit any of the property of the broker. Any assistance given to the pawn in this way by the broker required the assent of the broker's son.

At Onitsha Olona the amount for which a pawn would be given was £1 15s. for a small boy or £2 for a big boy and about twice as much for a girl. A sick pawn could not be replaced, nor could work days missed owing to sickness be reckoned against the pawn. If a pawn died three years of grace were allowed, If a pawn played truant a knot was tied in the cord, and the value of the day's work was reckoned at 420 cowries, that is 1½d. The knot had to be shown on the same day to the pawner, who had to pay for the sum total of the knots in addition to the debt.

At Okpanam where a boy was pawned for from 15s. to 25s., the day's work was reckoned at 4d. If a boy ran away, no money was claimed for the lost days, but a complaint would be made to the ǫkpala of the ẹbo when he was found.

At Ala the pawn worked for himself one day and for the

broker on two days. He was, of course, free to do as he pleased on the rest day. The pawn might live in his own house or in the creditor's house. A sick pawn who had worked well would be helped by the creditor, in other words the debt would be reduced. This might also be done if the pawn died, in which case his umunna would bury him and pay the debt. If a pawn absented himself persistently without reasonable cause, no addition could be made to the debt, but complaint would be made to the head of the pawn's umunna and repayment of the debt demanded. If the pawn ran away 15s. could be added to the debt. The broker might help the pawn to marry a wife, and in all cases except theft help him to pay his fines without reckoning the sum paid as part of the debt.

At Ibuzọ if the pawn died, the debt was extinguished; but the information was rather contradictory, for it was stated that children were always pawned to people who had no children and could adopt them ; on the other hand if the pawn died he was buried by his father. An idle boy could be sent home and the money demanded back, but no charge could be made for the lost days. If the pawn, on the other hand, showed good will, a wife could be procured for him, and he would remain in the family of the broker. In that case the money would never be repaid.

At g ashi the rule about lost days was the same. A satisfactory servant could be rewarded with a wife. At Oboluku if a man pawned himself and died in the broker's house, the debt was extinguished. If, however, he worked for the broker without living in his house the reverse appears to have been the case. A woman or girl invariably went to the broker's house. A knot was tied for a lost day and 140 cowries reckoned for it. If a child were pawned for £2 10s. or more, he or she went to the broker and worked every day. If the sum were less, the child had two days free and lived with its father.

At Idumuje Uboko a man would sometimes pawn himself to procure a wife, whom he could leave with her father or take with him to the broker's house. If he died before the debt was paid three years' grace were allowed, after which a new pawn had to be given or the debt paid. The missed days were reckoned at 140 cowries for boys and 200 cowries for girls.

At Ukunzu the number of days' work a week exacted from a pawn varied according to the sum raised. For 5s. one day's work, 25s. two days, for £2 10s. three days. Missed days were reckoned at one ngugu and marked with knots which were shown to the umunna of the pawn. The pawn might live in the broker's house, but might stay in his own house if he had a wife. If a pawn died the umunna would repay in three years. A good worker might be forgiven part of his debt or receive other favours. At Ukunzu a girl served every day and lived with the broker.

At Obọmpa the sum raised might be as much as £5. If a man pledged himself he built a house near the broker. For less than seven bags he got two days a week free, for more than seven bags only one, i.e., the rest day. The umunna were called as witnesses if days were missed, but there was no fixed sum per day. If the pawn died the money was lost ; he was buried by his people. A pawn might be wholly released in consideration of good work, or, if he preferred, he could remain and marry the broker's daughter, in which case the ordinary bride price was payable.

At Ezi a child which died below the age of 10 was buried by the father, but the debt was not extinguished. If he had been pawned some time repayment was not enforced. A young man of 20 had two days for himself. One ngugu was reckoned for a lost day.

At Obompa an exceptional rule prevailed to the effect that if the pawn stole, presumably from the broker, the debt was considerably increased.

In addition to persons, animals, trees, crops, or valuable objects might be pledged. The ordinary rule was that a pledged object could be used by the broker exactly as if it were his own property. A creditor was permitted to use a pledged object even to the extent of completely wearing it out, unless negligence could be proved in the use [of the object. The fact that it was worn out did not extinguish the debt. On the other hand, if the pledged object could not be produced, in however decrepit a condition, when the debt was repaid, it had to be replaced to the satisfaction of the debtor.

Thus at Qkpanam a gun could be used by the broker. If it burst or were otherwise spoiled, he would hang it up, and no compensation could be claimed by the debtor, who remained responsible for the money. The broker, however, had to show the damaged gun to the owner. If he did not do this, or if he used the broken pieces, another gun, presumably a good one, had to be handed to the owner when he repaid the money.

At Ala, on the other hand, a gun which could not be pawned for more than 5s., if it were spoilt and then lost, was not replaced, but half the debt was reckoned as extinguished. Cloth, on the other hand, which was pawned at half cost price, had to be replaced if it were spoilt and lost.

At Ezi, ivory anklets which were worn out by fair wear and tear in the broker's possession were not necessarily replaced, but might be handed over.

At Qkpanam, if a pawned object was stolen, the rule was that the owner had to be informed. If the thief were found, both owner and broker joined in seizing the property of the thief. The broker would not worry the pawner for repayment of the debt, but no compensation would be payable for the lost object.

At Onitsha Olona, if a pawned object were stolen by an unknown thief, the debt was extinguished and no compensation was payable.

At Ezi, on the other hand, if a pledge were stolen it had to be replaced or paid for, and the owner remained responsible for his debt. If the thief were found, the holder of the object received the compensation.

Where animals were pledged, the young produced after the pledging were usually regarded as the property of the broker. This was the case at Okpanam, Onitsha Olona, and Ezi. If the pledged animal died the owner received the body and remained responsible for the debt at Okpanam. At Onitsha Olona the meat was divided and the debt was extinguished. At Ezi the rule was the same, but the body might be left with the broker in satisfaction of the debt. In a few towns animals were not pledged. This was the case at Ala.

Trees.—Trees, as a rule, could be freely pledged except where they were of small value, as in the case of plantain and banana, which were usually sold. Where the tree is, as is often the case, on the land of another, free access is permitted. If the tree dies the common rule is that the debt is extinguished; but the wood of the tree goes to the broker. The produce of a pawned tree goes to the broker, but at Ala, singularly enough, the owner and not the broker was responsible for seeing that the nuts are not stolen. At Ala, if a third person fells the tree he makes himself responsible for the debt. If the tree falls into a pit it may be replanted by either broker or debtor, whichever was the nearer. A plantation of oil palms may be pawned only by the ọkpalẹbo, and then only after a meeting of the ẹbo has been held. If they could not or would not lend him money he was free to act. The ọkpalẹbo, however, may pawn part of a plantation on behalf of a third person. A young man, for example, may appeal to the ọkpalẹbo for money to marry a wife, and if the ẹbo agrees, the money may be raised on the plantation.

VIII.—TECHNOLOGY.

FARM.—It has been mentioned under Land that the farms are common property except during the time that they are actually in cultivation. The ordinary procedure is for the idumu or the umunna to go out in a body on a day fixed beforehand and mark out in common the area where they propose to make farm. The first proceeding is usually to cut a long central road or path, and off this are cut cross paths. The men then select plots according to seniority, and it is often arranged that the four senior men of the group which makes farm on a certain spot shall take the end plots, because, if they are ravaged by animals, they have more able-bodied men to watch the farm and wage war against the foe.

In Asaba, each obwe or idumu decides where it will plant, but two, three, or even four may join together and go to a certain spot before the decision is reached. The young men have probably been on the look-out for a suitable spot. Large plots, known as okpukpa, are divided off by paths, and the head chief of each idumu chooses one; but if the idumu is large, they may get five or six okpukpa. The size of the okpukpa were described to me as follows. It is 15 ufie long, and an ufie is said to be between three and four yards, and twenty nkpowa broad, that is, about eighty yards, though formerly the nkpowa appears to have been 6 yards. This estimate of size agrees on the whole with that given to me at Onitsha Olona. After these big sections have been assigned the okpukpa are cut up and divided either by mbe, which are sticks three feet high, or by digging small wedge-shaped holes known as abani, so that the small plots may be recognisable after the farm has been burned. If the land proves to be insufficient, the young men are instructed to make an additional okṗukṗa to divide and give to those who have no farm.

When this work is finished, each man goes to his farm to clear it. This takes about 28 days. Anyone who is behind-hand with his work is likely to get into difficulties, because if trees are felled they are likely to come across his plot and block his land before he has cleared it properly. Anyone who sees he is in danger of being left behind begs some of his friends for assistance.

Twenty-eight days after the completion of the clearing, if the spot cleared is big bush, they set fire to the trees and underwood. If it is an old farm, eight or ten days less may be required. When yams have been planted and the farm cleared of weeds, etc., the boundary between the different men's plots is usually made by corn stalks. This is about three months after the farm has been made, before that the mbe have marked it. Three kinds of ground are distinguished : ani olu, land near water, ubwẹni, a garden farm near the house, or not more than one hour away, and ugboko, the big farm, which may be as much as two hours away. Before the ground is cleared, its name depends upon how long it has been left since the last clearing. An area that has been cleared for 20 years is forest, Ugboko; if it is not 11 years old it is oifia or bush; if it is less than that, it is akwu or old farm.

If more ground has been cleared than is actually necessary, an overgrown portion may be left which is called onoli. This name is also given to a patch on which corn only is planted. If there is an alose on the farm the okumwọ will be left with bush round it.

At Isele Asaba, the young men go to. look at the bush before the ẹbo goes out to select the spot for the next farm, and anyone who has found a likely spot clears a small area and puts down crossed sticks. The ọkpalẹbo would be annoyed if, on summoning the ẹbo, he found that no one had done this. When the ẹbo go out to the bush, they dig the ground to see if it is good, and also look at the growth of the trees in the neighbourhood. Having decided on the spot, they cut the line known as okp̣ukp̣a. From the okp̣ukp̣a small furrows are cut on either side, known as mbe and oke. Plots are chosen by seniority, and anyone who finds that he is overburdened would ask others to help him. After the undergrowth has been cleared away, saplings are cut, which will be useful later, probably for yam sticks, and then the big trees. When all is dry the farm is burned and cleared.

At Onitsha Olona, the farm is divided up by mbe, four feet broad, and oke two feet broad. At Ala, a path known as okp̣ukp̣a is cut in the middle, and side paths, known a mbe, separate individual plots. Here the farms are said to be about 120 feet broad, and 200 yards long. Another estimate says 60 feet broad. If the latter is correct, the size agrees almost exactly with the estimate given me at Asaba.

At Ibuzọ, as at Ọkpanam and Asaba, the farms for the different years have names. These are as follows :

Akwu 1	...	...	Ezike.
„ 2	...	...	Isinta.
„ 3	...	...	Ogugu.
„ 4	...	...	Oloko.
„ 5	...	...	Odobwa.
„ 6	...	...	Ajamata.
„ 7	...	...	Ji onye.
„ 8	...	...	Kwafa.

They return to the same plot every eighth year, but they have one spare plot in case the farm is burnt too early.

At g ashi four okp̣ukp̣a are cut and then cross lines mmaji; each idumu gets a large plot and each umunna a subdivision. At Obuluku each idumu clears for itself, and then two cross roads are cut; each mbanua or umunna gets one of these small plots. After this oke or marks are put and each man clears his own plot; plots are measured by shouting to measure the distance.

At Idumuje Uboko, the method of making a farm is quite different. Radiating paths are cut from a centre, which is known as od odo ṅgwẹle, and when they have got a certain distance, branch roads are cut by individuals; after clearing a day is fixed for firing.

At Onitsha Ubwo, four cross roads known as okṗukṗa are cut, and the plots thus divided are known as imubwo. The four senior men of the umunna each get one of these plots, which are then subdivided.

At Ukunzu, centre lines are cut known as ịsimbe, and then side lines called oke ubwo. The plots are chosen on alternate sides according to seniority.

At Obọmpa no meeting is called but farm parties are arranged to clear certain areas. A passage is cut and a stick put across to show that the farm is claimed; this passage is known as ịsimbe or okwode. An ẹbwo stick is planted in esimbe and the first animal that they kill in the farm is offered to it.

Methods of farming differ to some extent in different places. As an example the methods of Isẹle Asaba may be briefly described. After the farm has been burnt and cleared, yams are planted, from four and a half to six rows, and corn near trees only. The yams are cut in pieces about the size of the two hands and planted in a trench known as obwa. A small heap of sand is put at the bottom, on this rests the seed, and after covering it in, dry leaves are put on the top to protect it from the sun. As soon as the small shoots begin to come out, the yam sticks are put in, but if there are two shoots on one root, one would be removed. The shoots are trained on small sticks known as alolo until they are big enough to reach the tall stick known as oni 4 feet high. A palm leaf|is used to tie the shoots to alolo and they are trained to climb counter-clockwise. When the shoots are tall they are bound round and begin to send out secondary shoots which are tied to each other and not to oni. If an oni is knocked down a fresh one is cut and put up.

The farm is weeded several times; the first time is known as afifia inu, the second as afifia obwenabo, and new corn is eaten during the second weeding. When the corn is getting dry the white yams are growing tubers and the seed is rotting. As it is supposed that the rotting of the seed may cause the new tubers, which are now about the size of a hand, to rot, the old seed is dug up. At the end of about 5 months some kinds of white yams are dug up and the subsequent treatment depends upon the species, for some are scraped and reburied and some are dug up once for all. After scraping each man puts a property mark on them, of which some illustrations are found on p. 183. Yams which have been reburied are dug up and sunned for a day and may then be stood on end by tens and twenties for about a month. After this in Asaba they are put in odo, that is, laid flat on logs in a heap 6 feet high; after this they are put in irhe. To make irhe in Isele Asaba thick saplings called ogidi are cut and planted in the farm; the place between them is called an abweli. Between these ogidi long cross sticks are tied with bush rope. These are known as obwalirhe and are three in number. Small sticks are now cut and jammed between the obwalirhe vertically and the yams are tied in rows ranging in number from 13 upwards. Mbubwa is the name of the row of yams.

The number of rows, ntoto, in each obwalirhe depends upon the size of the yams. There will be six ntoto of large yams, eight or nine of middle-sized yams, and ten of seed yams.

When the yams are dug up the heads are cut off with a sharpened stick and replanted so as to give seed. Palm leaves are cut and laid on the top and the sides of the irhe to shelter the yams from the sun. After two months the seed yams are dug up and mixed with alǫji, the small yams which have already been dug up for use in the next planting season. When they are clearing the bush the next year women come to the farm to buy yams. Twenty seed yams are sold at Isele Asaba for 1s., and from two to four mbubwa of other yams for 5s.

As to the quantities of yams planted, much depends of course upon whether sufficient ground is available and upon how large the family is. I was told at Asaba that a single man might plant 8,000 seed yams in addition to other crops,

N

such as koko yams, beans, corn, ǫkrǫ, pepper and ado. From these he would expect to get 6,000 good yams or more. For his father, mother and himself he would use 2,000 and the remaining 4,000 might be sold at a price varying from 1s. 4d. to 5s. for twenty and even higher prices might be paid if the yams were big. The total number of yams planted by a single household would vary considerably, and the Hinterland has a reputation of being less hardworking than Asaba.

At Ala I was told that a big farmer might plant 16,000 yams in a small year and 40,000 in a big year; a good worker should plant 200 yams a day. The size of the yams planted is regarded as having an important influence upon the size of the yams produced. Ikolǫji are planted to produce nnaji, alǫji for abolǫji, and so on. The names of the different sizes of yams differ to some extent in different places; the following are in use at Asaba. In brackets are given the names in use at Ala.

Big.	Moderate.	Medium.	Small.	Seed yams.
(a) nukuji.	(b) abwatanabo.	(c) ikolǫji.	(d) alǫji.	(e) akpalaji.
(nnaji.)	(abwolǫji.)	(„)	(„)	
3 for 1s.	4–5 for 1s.	8 for 1s.		Mixed with seed yams to plant.*

The sizes are approximately as follows:—

    (a) up to 25 lbs.
    (b) 5 or 6 are a heavy load for a boy of ten.
    (c) 10 are a full load for a boy of that age.
    (d) 25 „   ..   „   „
    (e) 40 „   „   „   „

I made a certain number of enquiries as to the amount of yams that could be raised on a given area, and there was on the whole a surprising agreement between the different estimates. At Onitsha Olona a normal farm, according to their estimate, would hold about 2,800 yams.

As regards work on the farm, a man is normally assisted

---

* Formerly 20 for 1 ngugu, now 20 for 6d.

by his sons, and if a man dies at Asaba all his sons would assist the eldest son so long as he treated them well. The children begin to cultivate farms at a very early age. I have seen a small boy's farm some 16 feet square close to a house, growing four or five different kinds of crops. At Asaba a son will get his separate farm, according to my informants, at the age of seven years and his mother buys seed yams for him. In addition to cultivating his own farm a son works every day for his own father until about the age of 24, but if he is married his father calls for his services only on oye day.

At Isele Asaba a boy does not begin to make his own farm until he is about 20; before that he only helps his father or his elder brother. At that age he would have his own small house and store his yams there. His father or elder brother would come and look at his yams, which are made up into rows of 12 or 13 and would sell rather more than half on the boy's behalf. It must be remembered that a boy of this age does not make his farm in order to support himself, for the father or elder brother, on whose farm he works regularly, supports him.

At Idumuje the rule is practically the same. All sons go to work on their father's farm and what they grow on their own farm they store separately. Until they marry they are supported by their father and they are at liberty to sell all yams from their own farms. Even if a son absents himself to work for a white man, his father will feed him on his return and give him seed yams.

At Ukunzu a boy works for his brother on oye and afọ days and is in return supported by his brother. What he plants on his own farm he can deal with as he pleases. He gives some to his mother, some he uses for himself, some he may allow his brother to sell for him. After marriage only one day's work is required from him.

It is possible to sell a farm with the yams in it, provided that the yam sticks have already been put in. Under stress of circumstances a man might sell half his farm at a price

N 2

depending upon the amount of weeding that has been done, and of course upon the species of yams. Broadly speaking, the farm on which the weeding has been done twice is worth double as much as the farm on which the weeding has been done once. From a portion of a farm containing 400 yams which are worth 5s. after the first weeding, it was estimated at Ubulubu that a man should be able to tie four abwẹli, worth from 15s. to 25s. according to the kind of yams. He could also get seed yams worth from 7s. 6d. to 10s., and the other crops known as if'ubwo would be worth 5s. Precisely how much work has to be done on a normal farm it is not easy to find out. At Ala I was told that they go to work at about 5.30 a.m. and have food ready at about 8.30 a.m. In the afternoon they have a second rest time and then the small children are given yams to take home to be cooked. The men return home about nightfall, food is brought by their wives, who have returned home earlier, and after a meal they go to sleep.

At Ubulubu the following was the estimate of the number of days' work after the planting, which might occupy a month, had been completed. Two spells, each 9 days, for weeding, and a total of 24 days for digging; about 4 or 5 days' work in addition would be required for seed yams and 3 or 4 days for tying the yams in irhe; 3 days for cotton; one day for koko yams; 3 days for akbaka and 9 days for pepper, making a total of about 65 days.

In addition to the crops mentioned above, which are frequently planted by women as well as men (especially koko yams), they also grow castor oil, tomatoes, various kinds of calabashes, leaves for soup, ground nuts, and finally, more important than any, corn. As regards corn, at Asaba it is stored in a special hut known as on·ogo. A bed of wood is made and the corn piled on it in triangular form. A normal pile of corn is 15 feet by 6 feet by 6 feet and would contain 10,000 heads.

At Onitsha Olona, corn is brought home when dry and may be laid on the akbata or drying place or hung from the ridge pole on ropes known as nkiko, which will take some 400 heads.

At Ala corn is sometimes put on the onogo bed or half may be put in the akbata with a fire underneath. Small circular granaries on the top of poles to prevent the attacks of rats are also used. These are known as ebili, or corn may be hung from a rope in the open air.

At Ibuzo corn is put on the nkiko beam in the house, which will carry 1,600 heads tied two together, and a fire is kept underneath.

At Idumuje, corn is hung from a rope in the house known as osodi oka and the heads are tied four together.

At Ani Qfo osodi is the name given to the two ropes for corn which hangs from the roof and the heads are tied in pairs. The area which will produce 1,200 yams will yield at the same time five osodi of corn.

At Obompa these ropes are known as osodi oka. Some leave their corn in the farm and some bring the heads home. Some eat all their corn when it is quite fresh and others will hang as many as seven ropes.

It has been mentioned above that women plant some of the crops. If a woman dies her husband takes her koko yams at Qkpanam, but gives some to ner children.

SPECIES OF YAM.

Name.		Dug up—	Lasts till—
1. *a.* ŏkû	red	Nov., Dec.	A year
b. „ ji oiča	„ but cut like white	Nov., early	March
2. Asokŏlo	white	Oct.	May
3. Alefûlu	..	..	July
4. Okbokŏlo		„ end	August
5. Agǎ		Sept., „	April
6. Ŏlŭ		Oct., „	September
7. Qle'		Sept., early	March
8. Oko (Onitsha)	„	Nov.	September
9. Okokwe „		..	July

Name.		Dug up—	Lasts till—
10. Ábì (Onitsha) white		Oct.*	August
11. Awụdu „	„	July†	March
12. Ẹbe „ and Igara „		June, July†	June
13. Abana—			
a. obute ọka (Igara) red		May†	Eaten at once
b. åsẹ̀lè	„ ani olu	June	May
	ani oiča		
c. agadǎga	..	Dec.	September
14. Onoku		Dec.	June
15. Alitu	„ ani olu	June	Eaten at once
16. Abanẹke	„ ani oiča	Aug., Dec.	June
17. Omafu	„ „	Dec.	August
18. Ọma ikbọ	„ „	„	June
19. Ačele			„
20. Oji odafe ukwe			May
21. Abananẽ	„ „	„	„

* After Christmas, or July, or March.
† After Christmas.

HOUSE.—The ordinary Asaba house ccnsists roughly of three parts, the ọgwa or front house standing in front of the house proper, and only intended for ceremonial uses and for sitting in; then comes the house proper, a large portion of which is open; and finally behind the house comes the women's house. In many places, a man, on reaching a certain status, has to build a kitchen, often known as ukoni, for he is not allowed to eat food cooked anywhere else.

A house called ụnabwa is built for a childless old woman who has no one to live with, and all her umunna take part in the work. A young boy of fifteen or sixteen will also build his own house, and in some towns he would also be buried there if he dies before marrying a wife. When he marries a wife, he frequently enlarges his bachelor's house till it is the proper size. In the first instance he has only two rooms, adani and okule, and a verandah, known as eba. A proper house is four times this size.

183

Yam Marks.

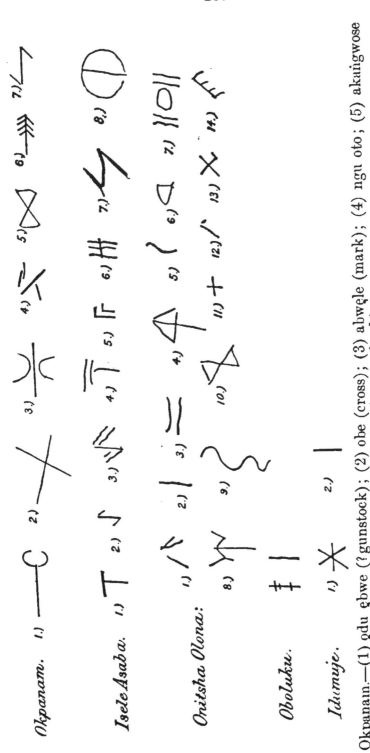

Okpanam.—(1) ǫdu ębwe (?gunstock); (2) obe (cross); (3) abwęle (mark); (4) ngu oto; (5) akaṅgwose (pepper pounder); (6) ǫdigu (palm leaf); (7) ngu (hook)

Isele Asaba.—(2) ngꞮꞮ; (3) ngꞮꞮ; (4) obufie; (5) isiokbo; (6) akala; (7) ngꞮꞮ; (8) osakṗwęlo.

Onitsha Olona.—3, 6, and 8 are calabash, the rest yams. (1) aba; (2) head; (3) abwęle (chest mark); (4) bow; (5) tail (of yam); (6) ufa (hole in the wall); (7) ainyębwe (nipple); (9) ijagwǫ (snake's path; (10) pepper pounder.

Idumuje.—(1) pepper pounder; (2) ofu arima.

PALM OIL.—The most important industry is the making of palm oil. The nuts are cut in March and put in a heap for five days; after this they are beaten to remove oiyilia, which is used for soap. After this they cut the separate bunches from the head and put them under leaves for four days. The nuts are then boiled and pounded in a mortar. One person collects the mashed husks, another squeezes it into a pot. The ball is then thrown back into the mortar. The nuts are wiped clean of oil with it and it is then squeezed again. The nuts are then cracked and the shells used for cooking, while the kernel is sold or used for nut oil. I enquired as to the quantity of oil produced and was told at Ala that a woman could get five mortars full from ten heads of palm nuts. Oil to the value of 1s. 3d. and kernels to the value of 1s. 6d. could be produced from this amount. If the kernels were used for making nut oil, there would be about four bottles, worth 4d. each.

PALM WINE.—Palm wine is prepared both from the *Raphia vinifera*, commonly known as bamboo, and from the oil palm. For the former, which is known as ǫgǫlǫ, a ladder is made up the tree, which should not be in seed, and the top is cut off. Then it is bored with a tool known as ize and the opening is covered with a leaf known as ǫlǫpǫ in order to prevent insects from penetrating it. A small opening is then made and a calabash is laid against it. The tree begins to produce wine three days after the operation and continues to yield it for two months, after which the tree is said to die.

Two kinds are prepared from the oil palm. The first is known as mainyankwo; this is made from the palm bud and is usually esteemed more highly. The branches are cleared away, leaving two small pieces as a support for the bud, which is bored in the middle. On the following day, after waiting 24 hours, a piece of wood is put across, and a spout of a reed passed through it, the other end being inserted into a calabash which is tied to a cross piece. The wine is collected in the morning and the opening in the bud brought slightly lower, otherwise the wine will not be sweet; a second supply is obtainable in the evening. Palm wine can be obtained in this way at any time, and the process is said to do no injury to the tree. The yield of palm wine is for about 16 days.

A more destructive method is to cut the roots of the tree on one side, and the palm wine thus obtained is known as ozu. The tree falls but part of the roots remain in the ground. The leaves are cleared away, and an opening in the trunk is made on the upper portion just where the leaves begin. Below this a small opening is made for the reed which drains the palm wine into the calabash. Every four days water has to be boiled and put into the hole at the top, after which the small hole has to be stopped; the object of this is to kill ants and insects. The tree continues to yield wine for 28 days; after this it is left for some three months until young leaves begin to sprout again. Palm wine of this kind is only obtained from young trees, and though the growth is doubtless injured, the tree is not completely killed; my informant, however, stated that the tree was spoilt.

In some towns, as has been shown in the section dealing with trees (p. 150), oil palms which grow in the neighbourhood of a man's house are his private property. In other cases, and perhaps more commonly, the tree is regarded as private property only so long as it is actually producing palm wine. As soon as the yield ceases it becomes again common property and anyone may tap it again as soon as it is ready to produce a further supply of wine.

FISHING.—A number of methods, more or less elaborate, are used on the banks of the Niger for catching fish. Some of these may be employed by a single individual, though he may perhaps require the assistance of a second man to paddle his canoe. Of this kind is the net known as ibolo which is some forty yards or more long and about two yards deep, and is kept up by floats. The casting net is said to have been learned from Yoruba or Gold Coast men. Another

net known as e d o requires two men to work it; they push
it under the water and lift it with the aid of sticks. A more
elaborate contrivance is that known as i k u m, which consists,
firstly, of a kind of basket which can be lowered into the
water by a cord. On the up-river side of this net is a fence
to cause a backwater; and when it is supposed that a fish
may be in the net one of the operators ascends a tower and
hauls up the net by means of a long rope to which small
pegs are attached at convenient intervals. His fellow stands
on the fence or in the water close to the net to secure the
fish if one is seen.

Various kinds of fish fences are used, some for shallow
water, others for deeper and broader streams. When the
river is falling, bundles of yam stalks are tied together
and put in the water near the edge, baited in the middle
with husks of palm nuts; this is done overnight. In the
morning the fisherman takes the bundles of yam stalks to
the shore and removes the fish. Spearing the fish by
torchlight is another method, and in waist-deep water a
man may wade and kill them with his matchet. Where
there is a patch which is stagnant, except at high Niger,
a fish poison may be used. A species of acacia is cut and
tied in bundles and left for three days. It is then cut small
and beaten with a stick and rubbed with the hands into the
lakelet. A rod and line are also used, but these are a recent
introduction.

STRING.—This is made from a plant known as i d e, which
is soaked and scraped (Pl. XIX) and then twisted on the
thigh.

PLATE XIX.

PREPARING "IDE" FOR MAKING STRING (OBOLUKU).

GIRL MAKING STRING (ALA).

IX.—MARKET.

Under ordinary circumstances the market in the Asaba district is held every four or eight days. Some towns have a daily market, usually held in the late afternoon. The hour for the big market varies to some extent, but it is usually in the late forenoon and goes on till about three. The market customs in Asaba are remarkable, in that each market, which is, of course, mainly attended by women, has an ọmu or market queen to preside over it. She deals with offences in the market such as theft or assault, sometimes with the help of the dignitaries of the town. She fixes prices and fines anyone who is guilty of breaking this law or of any of the things forbidden in the market. She takes dues of palm oil, and on certain occasions, when a sacrifice or other ceremony is required in connection with the market medicine, she may go out with her women to stop those coming to market and demand a percentage of their wares ; payment is, however, usually entirely voluntary.

In some places the market cannot begin until the ọmu arrives. If she does not come she must send a slave or one of the women to whom she has given a title. In some places she may punish the women of her town for non-attendance at the market and forbid them to go to distant markets instead of attending that of their own town.

Some of the towns on or near the waterside are remarkable, in that large markets known as ẹza, from the name of the founder of the first, are held at fortnightly or monthly intervals. They are attended by waterside people, who frequently come long distances by river, as well as by people from the interior. At the present day, owing to the existence of European factories perhaps, they have fallen into the background, but in the olden time they were evidently of great importance. The nzẹle had to send servants to the ẹza to help the ǫmu to keep order. The 13 ẹza in the year were divided as follows: Ezubo, Odogu, Onirhe, Odafe, Asabwa, Osodi, Ozǫma, Oinyǫbo, Okute, Onoi, Ǫmu, Iyase, and Isabwa, the first of the year being August 26th. In order to arrange the calendar, according to the statement made to me, a leap year, known as Ar'uku, was made once in four years, and Asabwa's ẹza, that is to say, the one held in January, was four days later than normally. Leap year is said to have been founded by Opeči, but it seems rather doubtful whether the astronomical knowledge of the natives was sufficiently exact to enable them to hit upon the number four as the one likely to give the best results. At the same time it must be remembered that it may have been adopted because the week is a four-day one, and it was important to keep the ẹza on the same day of the week, nkwǫ.

When the market had to be changed the Okute was the proper person to stop it; a wooden bell was beaten round the town and the announcement made. The ikei ani went to the doctors to enquire what alose should be in the new market; the adaisi sacrificed to it, and ǫmu then put down her calabash.

At Asaba the ẹza was held every 28 days, consequently they could reckon their year by the ẹza. People came from the Igara country bringing slaves, iron, potash, etc. A minor ẹza was held at the half month, but not so many people came. The ẹza at Asaba seems to have been stopped owing to the explosion of powder some 70 years ago.

In the case of the ordinary Asaba market the ǫmu had to put her own calabash down and take her seat before other women could take their loads off their heads. At the present day, owing, perhaps, to the fact that the Government market is not visited by many women because the site is unpleasing to them, the ǫmu does not fulfil her duties. In former days the ǫmu was entitled to take from each vessel of oil in the market about as much as would go into a tea cup. When a ceremony was to be performed in the town she could stop people coming to the market, and each person gave her a yam, a plantain, palm nuts, etc., to the value of about 1*d.*, which the ǫmu shared with her otu. The otu had to keep watch in the market and see that none of the prohibitions were violated. If a cock crowed in the market it went to ǫmu, though it could be ransomed at the price of 1*s.* If the wife of an ęze were knocked down, the adaisi, who was second to ǫmu, had to sacrifice a hen where she fell.

At Ǫkpanam the ǫmu sent her stool to the market as a signal to begin. She was not, however, compelled to remain as long as the market was open. To summon the ikci ani during the market for a big palaver she sounded an agogo or bell; she levied dues on the market women and made the market medicine; those women who refused to pay could be turned back. A rope was tied across the road and ǫmu sat down; each woman put her load down in order that selection might be made. Among the prohibitions in force in the market were the following :—

No cock was to crow.

No one was to fight in the market; if a matchet or knife were used the culprit might be fined one goat.

No woman was to come in with cords tied over her calabash.

If anyone sat down before ǫmu she could seize the whole calabash of the woman, but an Ǫkpanam woman or one related to the town would be warned only. Where a fine was not paid the ǫmu could seize the whole calabash.

At Isele Asaba money or contributions in kind were taken perhaps six times a year for the market medicine. Prices were settled by ǫmu, and anyone charging more would be fined. Ǫmu gathered in a calabash all articles sold in the market, as soon as she was appointed, and went with her otu (company) to the market. The prices at which she sold the various articles then were those established by law.

In former days, according to my informants, Isele Asaba had a market every day. At the present time markets appear to be held on two days in the week, but they recognise that it would be advantageous to have only one market day, and it might be desirable to make an effort to arrange the market days of a group of towns in such a way that each could get its fair share of trade.

At Onitsha Olona ǫmu fixed the prices and could confiscate the wares of anyone who attempted to sell at too high a price. She could make laws against sending yams to strange markets, but was not allowed to seize them, though she might stop the offender from going. If a woman ran from her husband to another town directly from the market the matter was one for ǫmu to deal with.

At Ibuzǫ it is noteworthy that if the young men cleaned the road of the market women each woman was compelled to give a leaf of tobacco.

At g ashi the ǫmu could fine for non-attendance at the market. The price of goods was fixed by sounding a bell in the streets and making an announcement. She could forbid women to go to distant towns to market. No penalty was payable unless the offender was caught in the act.

At Oboluku the women who went to market on the g ashi road had seven young men with them as guards. They hid in the bush till the end of the market, and when the market was over five more men came out and the women returned between these two bodies of men.

At Ukunzu the market was formerly on the Obǫmpa boundary, but a man was killed in a fight. Obǫmpa handed over a woman to settle the matter; after this a gun full of medicine was fired to draw the people from the old market to the market now held in the town.

GLOSSARY.

Abobo, mashed yam.

Ada, head woman of an ębo, etc.

Ada isi, head ada of a town.

Ado, a kind of tuber (?), which also bears edible seeds.

Adubwe, an alose.

Afǫ, a day of the week.

Ago; a person stands in the relation of ago to another person alive or dead, called their ci, and the ago is believed to be the reincarnation of the ci, or to be sent into the world with their help.

Aja, an offering put out on the road in a broken calabash, a basket of plaited palm leaves or other vessel, for witches, aj'omwo, etc.

Aǰ oifia, "bad bush," where objectionable corpses are exposed.

Alose, powers or demi-gods (?) (see Vol. I, p. 26, and Index).

Amosu, witch.

Anase, head wife.

Ani, the earth; regarded as an alose (deity).

Ani ęnu, the Hinterland and its language.

Ani oiča, the Asaba country and language.

Ani uku, ani of the whole town.

Aziza, a piece of palm fibre twisted and worn round the red cap of an ęze.

Bag (of cowries), five shillings; 16,000 cowries (small).

Ci, see Ago, nwago.

Dibia, doctor.

Ębo, quarter, the largest subdivision of a town.

Ebo, the man to whom a slave runs.

Ebwo, *Newboldia lœvis. Seem.*

Ęgo ony ama, informer's fee.

Ęke, a day of the week.

Ẹkwẹnsu, a dance held in the rainy season.

Erhi, *see* p. 19.

Eši, the same as erhi.

Ewu ose (ikẹṅga), goat killed when a theft has been committed.

Ẹze: (1) king; (2) holder of ẹze title; (3) chief or head.

Ẹze ikoḷọbia, head of the young men.

Ezi obulu, impluvium, open space in house.

Forbidding; a person is said to forbid an action, animal, etc., when it is, for ritual reasons, forbidden to him to perform the action, kill the animal, etc.

Hunger time, the period of scarcity of yams.

Ibanzu, "going into chalk," *i.e.*, retiring into the house for three days and rubbing chalk on the body at Iwaji.

Idumu or obwe, a subdivision of the ẹbo.

Ifejiọko, object used in the yam ceremonies, etc.

Ifẹnru, the dues payable to okpala, ọma, and other persons to whom service is rendered, also to the father-in-law.

Ifẹnza, kind of ordeal; flipping "medicine" in eyes of accused.

If'ọna, money for purchase of brass anklets.

If'ubwo, plants cultivated by women.

Igbo, ibo, slave; the name given to the tribes east of the Niger.

Igwe, a dance.

Ikei ani, the elders of the town.

Ikei ẹbo, the elders of the quarter.

Ikẹṅga (see vol. I, p. 39), a personal protective deity.

Inyi, sass-wood; used in the poison ordeal.

Irhe, the fence on which yams are tied.

Isomi, wife not purchased by the husband; her children belong to her own family.

Iwaji, festival of new yams.

Iyi, an alose on which an oath is taken; often a wooden dish with chalk, stones, etc., on it.

Ji ogige, one of the dues payable to the mother-in-law.

Mbannu, a bag of salt.

Mbuazu, a large dried fish.

Mbwa, " friend "; the lover of an idẹbwe.

Mwanọ, annual sacrifice to ancestors.

Mwọ, dead ancestors.

Ndi ẹze, plural of ẹze.

Ndičie: (1) at Asaba, the eldest men in the town; (2) at Isele Asaba, the men who have not taken ọkpala title; (3) ancestors.

Nẹmoniča, an alose (deity).

Ngugu, 780 cowries, 3d.

Nkata tree, *Raphia barombiensis*, Faub.

Nkpese, the first title at Asaba, Okpanam, etc. (see p. 54).

Nkwọ, a day of the week.

Ntoto, a " rope " of yams, 13 or more in number.

Nwada, a child born in town A of woman who was born in town B, is a ṅwada of town B.

Nwago, see Ago.

Nwunyẹze, wife of ẹze.

Nze: (1) the same as ọkpalẹbo; (2) the object which represents the ancestor of the ẹbo.

Nzẹle, dignitaries, *see* p. 40.

Nzu, see p. 15.

Obi, head chief.

Oboku, an alose.

Obu, a man who killed a human being **or** dangerous animal.

Obwe, see Idumu.

Ọbwọ, see p. 45.

Ọbwọdọ, a ceremonial spear used in dancing.

Odo, *Dissotis rotundifolia triana*.

Ọfọ (see Index), a small piece of wood used for ceremonial purposes, which often represents the father in ancestor worship.

Ọgwa, " front house," an open building in front of the house proper.

Oiyilia, the stem of a head of palm nuts.

Ojuku, a kind of oil palm tree.

Okei, the oldest man in the town or quarter.

Qko, 140 cowries.

Qkpala: (1) the head of the ẹbo, idumu, or umunna;
(2) the oldest person in the family of father or mother:
(3) see p. 57, the name of the title corresponding to ẹze
at Isẹle Asaba and elsewhere.

Okpukpa: (1) plot for farm; (2) path in farm.

Okwa, breadfruit; *Treculia.*

Olinzẹle, the same as Nzẹle.

Qma, the relationship between a person and his ọkpalanne
(see p. 51), male or female.

Qmalẹgwe, man who has killed a human being or dangerous
animal.

Qmu: (1) market queen; (2) young palm leaves.

Qmụnọ, image of woman's mother (?) in her kitchen.

Onotu: (1) the same as Nzẹle; (2) young men (*see* p. 43).

Orhăi, a shrine more especially associated with a doctor, in
which are kept the various alose.

Orhẹne, priest.

Qsisi, a staff used in the cult of ancestors; the same as Bini
uxure.

Osŭ, an iron staff used in the cult of Osŭ at Benin City and
Oniča Olona.

Otu rhaza, the four ọbwọ immediately below the ndičie
at Asaba.

Oye (olie), a day of the week.

Oziza, part of the bride price.

Ozo, a blacksmith.

Patrilineal, tracing descent in the line of the father.

Tutu, a kind of bush rope.

Ukho, the raised mud seat used by a man who has taken a
title.

Uke: (1) a ceremony performed for a girl near the age of
puberty; (2) the evil which is supposed to be expelled
by the ceremony and driven into the bush; (3) the
ọbwọ at Asaba immediately below a man's own
ọbwọ.

Ukoni, separate kitchen for cooking the food of a titled
man.

Umuago, plural of ṅwago.

U̇munadi, the dead people of an ẹbo.

Umunna, sept, the smallest subdivision of the town, com-
posed of the people who trace their descent to a
common male ancestor, and recognise a tie of kinship
closer than that between persons of the same idumu
or ẹbo.

Umwada, plural of ṅwada.

INDEX.

Social unit, 161.

Son's rights over trees, 151; work for father, 179.

Strange markets, visiting, 190.

Stranger, in farm land, 147; and land, 145 *sq.*; property of 136.

Step-sister, 129.

String, 186.

Succession to obi, 40.

Suicide, 43; of murderer, 88 *sq.*

Suitor, choice of, 63.

Taking charge, 157.

Theft, 57, 158, 171; by slave, 125; by woman, 100.

Thief, finding, 108; *see also* Ordeal.

Titles (grades), 54 *sq.*; idębwe takes, 78.

Totemism, 13, 17, 26, 30.

Towns, plan of, 4; subdivisions of, 7.

Tort, 110.

Traditions, 8.

Trading, 130, 137 *sq.*

Trees, 149 *sq.*; felling, 172; pawning of, 172; pawned, death of, 155; as temporary private property, 149, 153.

Trespass, 110.

Trials, 38.

Tribute, annual, to Benin, 39; (rent) for land, 148.

Twins, 18.

Udo, 48, 55.

Uke, 32, 48.

Ukoni (kitchen), 54, 182.

Umunna, 61, 64, 66, 141, 158, 161; mates, rights of, 153, 162.

Umunadi, 27, 82.

Ụnabwa, 182.

Uruči, 27.

Virginity, 59, 65, 67.

Vulture, 23, 25.

HARRISON AND SONS, Printers in Ordinary to His Majesty, St. Martin's Lane.

ND - #0081 - 210323 - C0 - 229/152/14 - PB - 9781331885641 - Gloss Lamination